PASHA'S JOURNEY

Dennis Morton

Published By

A Curious Crow

Pasha - Sibbey
Off Mafeting
Bosuto Lan
Basutoland

ABOUT THE AUTHOR

Dennis Morton, the author of 'Pasha's Journey, 'has led a life less ordinary. From being conscripted into the South African army in 1979 to managing oil exploration projects internationally, his journey has spanned continents and causes. However, it was his work standing shoulder to shoulder with nomadic tribes in Africa – fighting to stop destructive oil ventures – that truly defined his life's mission. Now a community activist and keen allotmenteer, Dennis brings his passion for storytelling and advocacy to the page. A photographer at heart and a poet by nature, 'Pasha's Journey' is his first published novel, blending the spirit of adventure with the deep-rooted activism that has shaped his extraordinary life.

A Note on Historical Language and Terms

In *Pasha's Journey*, you will encounter language, ideas, and attitudes reflective of the colonial era—some of which may be considered offensive or outdated today, particularly regarding race, empire, and power.

This historical novel is set in a time when such terms were woven into everyday speech, reinforcing colonial authority, oppression, and discrimination. To sanitize that language or soften the realities of the era would risk erasing history's brutal truths and diminishing the struggles of those who lived through them.

As the author, I want to make it clear: I do not endorse these views. Their inclusion is not meant to perpetuate them but to honestly portray the world as it was. This is a story of resistance, injustice, and survival—one that seeks to illuminate forgotten histories rather than obscure them.

I encourage you to read with critical awareness, reflecting on how past injustices continue to shape the present. By confronting history truthfully, we ensure that the voices of those erased by empire are not forgotten.

Thanks for joining me on this journey.

Dennis

"Beneath the wings of midnight,
Where time and fate collide,
The Crow weaves what is forgotten,
Into what must yet arise."

THE BELL'S TOLL

An early morning fog had invaded Glasgow, choking out the light and harbouring the cold. It was a Tuesday.

A crowd had gathered outside the northern wall of Duke Street Prison, a puzzle of anxious spectators dressed in black. Their breath rose into the still air like pale ghosts. The living wavered between morbid curiosity and a hunger for justice.

Two flagpoles on top of the northern wall pierced the grey sky. A crow perched on the wall, its feathers dark as tar, its eyes gleaming like wet stone.

A damp Union Jack hung limply on the second pole, heavy from the overnight rain.

Duke Street Prison stood heavy with history, its stone walls steeped in the weight of those who had come before. In one of its cold, narrow cells, a young Basuto sat unmoving, his dark eyes fixed ahead—calm, steady, unreadable. A Sesotho Bible rested on his lap, his fingers lightly tracing its worn cover. Though his hands trembled slightly, he gave no sign of feeling the chill that crept through the floor and into his bones.

In the days leading up to this moment, fear had abandoned him. With no family to mourn his loss and no one to plead for his life, he felt completely alone. Abandoned by a world indifferent to his existence, he discovered a strange peace—a quiet acceptance of the end that loomed just beyond the iron door of his prison cell.

A mournful bell tolled through the chilled air, silencing the crowd. The sound was low and sombre, as if the earth was weeping.

With a jarring screech, the iron door of the prison cell groaned open. Two familiar faces appeared—the guards. The young Basuto stood up and walked toward them. His steps were measured, and his movements deliberate, as if he had rehearsed this short journey many times.

The procession moved through the narrow halls, their footsteps muffled by the thick silence that filled the prison. The sheriff led the way, followed by the prison doctor and two warders. The barefoot young man walked at the centre, flanked by men who seemed more shadow than flesh. The air was thick with quiet sorrow. Behind them, a priest followed in silence.

Inside the execution chamber, the noose hung motionless.

As he entered the dim chamber, the Basuto calmly glanced around, noting the solemn faces of the few gathered there. Not a word was spoken to disturb his last thoughts.

He stepped up to the makeshift platform, his toes touching the chalk line where he had rehearsed to stand. The executioner bound the prisoner's ankles and then placed a white hood over his head, shrouding him from the world. The noose was slipped around his neck, firm and final, each action a solemn ritual of death.

Outside, the crowd fell into a hushed silence, their eyes fixed on the flagpole that pierced the gloomy sky pressing against the prison's stone walls. For a moment, the world held still.

A solitary figure watched from the edge of the crowd, his expression unreadable. He was tall, and his face was obscured beneath the brim of a wide Homburg hat. He turned a pencil in his fingers, his notebook pressed under his arm, pages scrawled with careful notes. Beside him stood a man with a Goerz Anschütz camera; for now, they remained silent witnesses rather than reporters.

As the bell tolled its final note, the journalist bowed his head in understanding and quiet respect.

Henry Albert Pierrepoint pulled the lever at that last bell peal before the bell echo could start. There was a rattle of bolts, and the trapdoor dropped. The rope snapped taut in a movement too quick to capture a breath, a sudden end to a life.

At precisely one minute past eight, the halyard on the second flagpole tightened, and a small black ball spluttered up the pole. When it reached the top, it burst open like a dark flower blooming in the cold dawn, serving as a silent, irrefutable mark that life had ceased, never to return.

The crowd, their curiosity sated, drifted away, swallowed by the busy streets.

The crow took flight, its dark wings cutting the sky. It circled once, an inked omen against the clouds—then vanished into the grey.

Though the young Basuto's life had ended, his story was just beginning.

"Beneath the northern wall of Duke Street Prison, a patch of grass lay flat with the morning's dampness. In the shadow of stone, the condemned were buried—each life reduced to a marker, worn by time and neglect.

A freshly dug grave awaited, its dark soil heaped beside it like a silent witness. The headstone stood ready, its surface smooth and final: Pasha Liffey, 1880–1905. The letters were sharp and clear.

Two men lingered over the hollow, their shovels idle, their boots sinking into the soft ground. They watched the grave in stillness, their presence as silent as the earth beneath them. Overhead, a crow perched on the prison wall, its feathers gleaming in the dim light. It shifted, uneasy, then spread its wings and rose. Its cry cut through the silence.

Soon, the body would be brought here. The grave would close, the stone would be placed, and the patch of earth would return to its quiet patience, as it always did."

ECHOES ON HAMILTON STREET

S kipping ropes slapped against the pavement on Hamilton Street, just a stone's throw from where Pasha Liffey was said to have committed a heinous crime. The girls playing there were too young to remember it—too young, even, to have heard more than whispers. Yet their voices carried the echoes of an old tale, woven into the rhythm of their skipping song, a haunting, sing-song chant:

> *"Pasha Liffey's dead,*
> *Lying in his bed.*
> *He cut her throat with a knife and fork—*
> *Now Pasha Liffey's dead."*

Their voices carried the dark rhyme down the street, turning it into a playground song as familiar as any rhyme about witches or haunted woods. The children laughed, oblivious to the tale behind the words. For the older folks, the chant was a ghost of the past—Pasha's shadow lingering over Larkhall, refusing to fade.

Nearby, parked on the corner, was an ice cream van, its motor humming quietly under the warmth of the summer evening. The chimes of its tune had drawn the children over, and they clustered around, clutching sticky pennies and tuppences, grinning as they waited for their cones of vanilla swirled high. The smell of waffle cones and melting cream hung in the air, mingling with the earthy scent of the street.

Mrs Findlay watched from her window, the chant pulling her back to whispers long ago. She had first heard Pasha's name as a child, murmured with fear and fascination. Now, decades later, the echoes remained—woven into the town's bricks, its narrow closes, and the skipping games of children who had no idea what they were singing. Even then, there had been dark murmurs—words she had not understood, carried by the wind from the adults who gathered on the corners, shaking their heads and muttering about "that poor lad."

The town had tried to move on. New estates had sprung up, rows of concrete flats lined the edges of old streets, and teenagers with a new edge were starting to put their faith in rock and roll rather than the ghosts of Larkhall's past. But certain things stayed, rooted too deeply to be shaken off by the slow march of time.

For Larkhall, Pasha's name had become both legend and curse, spoken in quiet tones by the older generation and sung loudly, rhythmically, by children who skipped in the same lanes he had once walked. The name surfaced in conversations at kitchen tables and in family living rooms, where parents, uncertain of how much to share, would hint at the tale, careful to keep the shadows of the past at arm's length.

Some folks avoided Hamilton Street altogether, unwilling to pass by the spot where it had happened. They carried a quiet superstition, a conviction that some pieces of history were best undisturbed.

In the pubs on Carlisle Road, Union Street, and even at Merryton station, the tale would occasionally be resurrected with a clink of beer glasses and a whispered dare. "Remember Pasha?"

someone would ask, their voice blurring fear and fascination. And the stories would spill out—a jumble of half-truths, fragments, and the occasional hushed suggestion that it had all been a setup. "He was innocent," some would say, their words heavy with doubt, their voices low, as if the walls might be listening. Others claimed they had seen his ghost, a figure slipping in and out of the shadows, watching from the corners, his presence as much a part of the town as the bricks of the Dykehead Colliery.

But for all the mystery and hushed tones, the memory of Pasha was most alive in children's voices—echoes of a crime they could not understand, a rhyme that belonged to them as surely as any other in their games. The words took on a life of their own, and with each passing year, they would be handed down to new generations who might know nothing of Pasha yet would sing his name just the same.

Larkhall wore its past on its sleeve, and in 1966, the lines between past and present remained blurred. The townsfolk felt it in the air, a strange tension between memory and progress. The young looked toward Glasgow, where they could find work or adventure; the old kept one eye on the familiar streets and the other on the past they could never entirely leave behind.

As the sun dipped behind Larkhall's sandstone cottages, the children's voices floated on the evening air—Pasha's name, weightless yet inescapable, drifting like leaves on the wind.

THE TRADING POST

Pasha shivered, pulling his oversized jersey tight as he lingered outside Fraser's Trading Store in Mafeteng. A pale sun pressed against the thick morning mist, its glow weak against the cold. Frost clung to the grass and thatched rooftops, brittle and gleaming. It was 1890. Winter in Basutoland carved silence into the land, its beauty edged with cruelty.

Frasers had opened for the day, and already, the area was humming with activity. Traders and villagers converged at the store, their breaths clouding the icy air. The heady aroma of tobacco and paraffin, laced with the earthy scent of maize meal and the sweetness of sugar, escaped in wisps each time the heavy wooden door swung open. A brindle dog, ochre with dark streaks along its flanks, lay sprawled on the store's porch. As the crowd thickened, it stretched, rose stiffly, and limped through the gathering. It paused by Pasha, meeting his gaze with quiet kinship before drifting into the morning's bustle.

On the store's corrugated roof, a pair of Cape Turtle doves shuffled restlessly - their feathers fluffed against the cold. Nearby, a brood of hens and a rooster scratched and pecked at the ground, their gentle clucking adding a soft rhythm to the morning melody.

Pasha gazed over the scene, soaking in the sights and sounds. Villagers wrapped in thick blankets moved about the trading post. At the same time, Basuto ponies stood tethered nearby, their steady breaths forming small clouds as they shifted calmly like sentries on watch. Children dashed around, laughing despite the cold, while elders gathered in warm circles, their voices low and focused, deliberating and negotiating like generals discussing battle plans.

The trading store was more than just a place of commerce—it was the beating heart of Mafeteng. Inside, shelves brimmed with neatly folded Basuto blankets, their indigo and earthy browns stacked high. Sacks of maize meal lined one wall, while paraffin tins near the entrance caught the dim light. Heavy iron ploughs, hoes, and sickles hung from beams, ready for the next planting season. Tin cups, metal pots, and kettles gleamed alongside sacks of coffee beans and tobacco twists. Coils of rope, spools of thread, and bundles of cloth filled the shelves—a promise of comfort and utility.

For Pasha, Fraser's felt like an anchor in the vastness of his world. He watched the trading of maize, sugar, and tobacco with a hunger that went beyond his empty stomach; each item promised a brighter day.

A light tap on his shoulder brought him back. He turned to find the storekeeper, Mr. Fraser, whose familiar face crinkled into a warm, knowing expression. This kind look spoke of years spent in the village, a lifetime of early mornings and hard-earned understanding. Fraser gestured for him to come inside, his smile both an invitation and an unspoken promise of something more—perhaps work—and the chance to earn just a little extra.

Pasha hesitated, then nodded. The store's light and warmth beckoned him. As he stepped inside, a quiet anticipation filled him, the kind that overtakes a person on the brink of a small but precious victory. Outside, the mist began to dissolve as the first clear shafts of sunlight broke through, smearing their golden light across the village.

The brindle dog watched Pasha disappear inside, its tail flicking once before it limped toward the children. As it wove through the morning bustle, each step quiet with resilience, Pasha soaked in the store's warmth, feeling the faint tug of hope. Outside, the village hummed with life, and with quiet resolve, Pasha was ready for whatever the day would bring.

SHADOWS ON THE ATLANTIC

Cape Town, 1899. The docks rang with the clatter of crates, the shouts of labourers, and the sharp cries of seagulls. The March air hung thick with salt and sweat as dockworkers moved with steady efficiency, preparing for journeys that sparked dreams of fortune and adventure.

A crow swept above the harbour, a dark crescent against the pale dawn. It circled once, then vanished into the sky.

March 25 was a Saturday, a day infused with hope and uncertainty. The SS Goth loomed ominously at the wharf—a hulking iron leviathan, its hull reflecting the morning light with an unsettling gleam. More than just a vessel, the ship was a creature of the British Empire, poised to swallow the strange assembly of lives gathered before it. Anticipation crackled in the air, thick with the thrill of the unknown. This voyage promised no comfort, no luxury, only the murky promise of what lay beyond the vast Atlantic.

On the stone quayside, animals from distant lands stood crammed into temporary pens or confined within crates, their breaths shallow and uneasy. Hundreds of horses and ponies stamped and shifted, wide-eyed with trepidation, ears flicking back at every creak and clang. Elephants, tethered by thick chains, lumbered slowly in makeshift corrals; low rumbles resonated from their massive chests like echoes of ancient thunder reverberating through the earth. Lions paced in iron cages, their fierce amber eyes sharp and unyielding, each twitch of their tails betraying the restlessness within. Leopards, zebras, baboons, and eight Indian tigers —all under the wary eyes of dockhands—awaited their turn to be swallowed by the ship's dark hold.

One by one, the animals were lifted aboard, swallowed by the iron hull. The cranes groaned under their weight, swinging elephants aloft. Their mournful trumpets rang out over the harbour, fading as they disappeared below deck.

The caged lions were swung over the quayside, their massive frames shifting with the sway of the ropes. Eyes once sharp with dominance now stared blankly as they disappeared below deck, swallowed by the darkness of the ship's hold.

The zebras stood motionless, their ears flicking at the sudden clang of iron. Ponies, tethered tight, rolled their eyes in silent distress, their bodies rigid as the handlers yanked their leads. They smelled fear—thick and cloying, rising from the cramped crates and trembling limbs around them.

The leopards crouched low at the bottoms of their cages, pressed against the cold metal. A whip cracked, a chain rattled, and one by one, they were heaved aboard, their sleek bodies reduced to cargo.

Then came the human cargo. Men, women, and children from Basutoland, Matabeleland, Zululand, Swaziland, Transvaal, and the Orange River Colony stood in silent lines, their faces unreadable, their fate decided long before they reached this place. There was no struggle, no protest—only the quiet weight of inevitability. Some had abandoned their homes, others coerced, drawn into a world where they would become exhibits, curiosities under a foreign gaze. Each figure carried the weight of history, their spirits intertwined with the lands they were leaving behind.

Pasha Liffey, a young Basuto, leaned against the harbour's stone wall, watching the lines of men, women, and children shuffling toward the waiting ship. Behind him, a faded recruitment poster flapped weakly in the breeze, its bold lettering still commanding attention despite its age.

"Savage South Africa! A Sensational Exhibition of Native Life!
Wanted: Able-bodied Men from Basutoland and Matabeleland!
Afrikander Girls—Good-looking and Slightly Coloured!"

He had answered that call. He had stood before a recruiter, signed his name, and he was now ready to board the SS Goth bound for a world he could barely imagine. A promise of opportunity, of adventure, of London's dazzling streets—those had been the words that lured him. But standing there now, watching those who had also taken the bait, some eager, some uncertain, he saw it for what it was. Not an invitation, but a transaction. A showman's trick, dressing up hardship as spectacle, turning flesh and blood into props for the empire's illusion.

Frank Fillis prowled the docks, every step purposeful. This was his craft, his theatre. Each beast, each man, was a carefully chosen piece in his grand illusion, arranged with the precision of a showman. To Fillis, mystery was the greatest lure—the less his audience knew, the more they would imagine. And in that unseen space, his legend grew, whispered through the streets of London long before he even arrived.

It was Pasha's turn to board. Ahead of him, a steady line of passengers shuffled towards the desk, murmuring their names to the wiry clerk who barely looked up. He sat hunched over a ledger, spectacles slipping down his nose, his pen moving swiftly, recording each name with brisk, precise strokes. Fillis. Kruger. Williams. Each name carefully inscribed, then stamped with "First Class."

Then came the thick dividing line—bold, unmissable, running straight across the page like a barrier. Below it, the heading read "Steerage Class." No names followed. Just numbers. Twenty-three coloured men and boys. Five coloured girls. 148 native men. Four children. No identities. No passengers. Just inventory.

A man ahead of Pasha adjusted the cloth bundle slung over his shoulder, shifting his weight as he stepped forward. His boots were worn, soles patched with scraps of leather. Behind him, a young girl clutched a wooden doll missing an arm, her free hand gripping the hem of her mother's dress. The mother kept her eyes low, murmuring something under her breath—a prayer, perhaps, or a quiet plea to remain unseen.

Pasha inhaled sharply as the clerk's pen hovered over the page, waiting. He stepped forward. The clerk didn't ask for his name. He simply dipped the pen into ink, prepared to add another stroke to the list.

Pasha stepped onto the deck. The harbour remained a blur of sights and sounds, lingering in the early light as he moved across the deck and reached the bulwark. The cries of seagulls mingled with the distant shouts of dockworkers, a final chorus of the world he was leaving behind.

With a deep, rumbling vibration, the engines roared to life beneath Pasha's feet. The ship began to edge out of the harbour slowly as if reluctant to leave the familiarity of the land behind. As it gathered speed, a veil of grey clouds drifted in, obscuring the bright sun and casting a shadow over the ship. The first cold drops of rain struck Pasha's skin. The drizzle spread, softening the view of the receding port.

As the SS Goth pushed deeper into the Atlantic, Cape Town softened, fading from view until only the open expanse of the ocean remained. The rain picked up, dancing on the water's surface.

The Atlantic rolled on, endless and indifferent, as the ship cut through the grey waves. It was well into the first day's journey when Pasha saw him—standing alone at the far end of the deck, a solitary figure leaning into the sea breeze. His back was straight, his shoulders broad, and his gaze fixed on the horizon as if he could see something far beyond the earth's curve. There was a stillness about him, a kind of silent authority that demanded attention without asking.

Pasha hesitated, feeling the chill of the ocean spray on his face, and then he walked forward, each step a little heavier as the distance between them closed. As he drew nearer, he could make out the man's features: dark eyes, deep and steady, framed by a face that seemed carved from stone. He carried an air of dignity.

The man remained still as Pasha approached, his gaze steady on the dark water ahead. Only when Pasha stopped beside him did he turn, eyes narrowing slightly, as if he had been expecting this conversation.

"You've crossed before?"

Pasha rested his hands on the railing, feeling the salt air on his skin. He glanced at the man beside him—Lobengula, though he didn't know that yet—then back at the shifting waves.

"Yes. England. Summer of '91."

Lobengula gave a thoughtful nod, absorbing the answer. "And now, you return?"

Pasha exhaled, his grip tightening slightly. "It seems I do."

A flicker of something—curiosity, recognition—passed through Lobengula's eyes. He turned slightly toward Pasha, his posture relaxed but watchful.

"And where is home?"

"Liphiring. Near Mafeteng. Basutoland."

Lobengula considered this for a moment before offering a measured nod. Then, extending a hand, he said, "Lobengula. Some call me Peter."

The name settled between them like a stone dropped into deep water, rippling outward. Pasha felt its weight at once. He had heard the whispers among the Matabele on the quayside—quiet, reverent murmurs of a Lobengula. A name tied to kings, to a past that had not faded, only shifted into shadow. They spoke of a man whose lineage still carried weight, whose history moved with him—silent, unseen, yet never forgotten.

The wind picked up, tugging at the edges of their clothes. They both turned back to the horizon. A silence settled, broken only by the groan of the ship's metal and the slow, relentless wash of waves against the hull.

Lobengula spoke first, his voice quiet but carrying against the wind. "How does a boy from Liphiring end up in England?"

Pasha glanced at him, then back at the shifting water. "Fraser. Douglas Henry Fraser. He ran trading stores in Basutoland. Took me on as a groom when I was ten."

Lobengula's brow furrowed slightly, turning the name over in his mind. He gave a slow nod. "A trader, then."

"Had money. Had connections." Pasha exhaled, watching the swirl of foam below. "He took me to Ipswich. Ten years, more or less. But I came back. Been here a year now."

Lobengula didn't press, just let the words settle between them, the ship's engines folding into the slow heartbeat of the Atlantic swells. The wind carried the scent of salt and something older—something that whispered of lost things, distances stretched thin across time and tide.

"You grew up around the Fraser stores, then?" Lobengula asked, his tone light but curious.

Pasha shook his head. "No. There was a mission near Liphiring. Reverend Édouard Jacottet ran it. I spent a lot of time there, learning what I could."

Lobengula repeated the name under his breath. "Jacottet. A missionary?"

"A good one," Pasha said simply. "Taught me things. Showed me a way of seeing."

Lobengula nodded again, absorbing it, but he said nothing. The quiet stretched. It was not uncomfortable. Just full.

Then, Pasha spoke again. "I've heard things about you."

Lobengula's eyes flickered, but he didn't look over. "Oh?"

"They say you're the son of King Lobengula."

A shadow passed over Lobengula's face, but he didn't flinch. He didn't confirm or deny it either. He just let it hang there, caught in the wind, like the pale moon beginning to rise over the horizon.

"And what do you think?" he asked finally. His tone was light, but there was something beneath it—something careful, watchful.

Pasha met his gaze. "I think some things are better left unspoken. Don't you?"

For a moment, Lobengula said nothing. Then, slowly, he smiled. A knowing smile. A tired one.

They turned back to the sea.

The SS Goth pressed deeper into the Atlantic, the wind shifting around them, carrying past and future alike. They stood side by side, not speaking, not needing to.

Above them, the crow circled again—a dark fragment of night—gliding silently into the clouds, bearing witness.

Pasha made his way down the narrow stairway, the vibration of the engines humming through the steel underfoot. The noise from the deck above—voices, footsteps, the clatter of rigging—faded away, swallowed by the deep, steady pulse of the ship engine pushing through the ocean.

At the bottom of the stairs, he stopped. The air was warmer and heavier.

Lanterns swung overhead, casting a flickering light over the scene—men and women resting in hammocks, some sharing quiet conversations, others staring off into the half-darkness.

It was a world of movement and noise, yet it felt closed off, as if the ship had swallowed these people whole, keeping them apart from the world above.

They were caught between two worlds—their lives suspended in the murky glow of the lanterns as the SS Goth carried them toward a new, uncertain future.

Pasha turned and moved back toward the narrow stairway. The voices of the Zulu, Basuto, Swazi, and Matabele followed him, rising and falling like the restless waves beyond the ship's walls. He had seen their world now—the hidden, crowded reality of steerage—and as he climbed back up to the deck, he carried a piece of it with him, the echoes of those voices settling into his memory like the roll of the endless Atlantic.

THE DAY THE DOCK TREMBLED

Southampton Harbour, April 19, 1899

The Biograph film camera stood like a sentinel at the quayside, its lens poised for history. It was an overcast Wednesday, and Southampton Harbour lay shrouded in mist. Through the shifting grey, the crowd strained for the first glimpse of the SS Goth, steaming in from Cape Town after twenty-six days at sea.

News of the ship's cargo had stirred the city's imagination— caged beasts from distant lands, Zulu warriors with fierce eyes, Boer commandos with stoic gazes, and Empire troops in polished boots. It promised spectacle, a glimpse of the unknown arriving on English soil.

The hull of the SS Goth emerged, its steel pressing through the fog. At first, a faint outline—then, as the mist curled away, its hulking form took shape. Coal smoke churned from its chimneys, the iron hull shifting and creaking as the ship eased into port. Excitement rippled through the crowd. The Biograph crew adjusted the camera focus while their director, William Kennedy Laurie Dickson, readied himself to capture this moment—the world's first moving spectacle on film.

Beyond the stacks of crates and shifting shadows, another figure watched. His Homburg hat was pulled low, shielding his face. A pencil rested on a worn leather notebook, its edges softened by years of use. He observed differently than the crowd. Where they saw marvels, he saw nervous dockworkers, wide-eyed children clinging to their mothers, and port authorities standing rigidly at attention—faces cast in shadow and mist.

The fog crawled across the docks, creeping alongside the ship, softening edges, blurring the theatre of the moment. Then, with a deep groan, the SS Goth came to rest.

Ropes were thrown. The gangplank thudded onto the dock.

The Biograph camera clicked and whirred, its mechanical eye focused on the scene unfolding.

A hushed murmur swept the crowd as the first shapes emerged from the ship's belly.

A massive elephant loomed on deck, silhouetted against the fog. Gasps followed as crates of lions were lowered onto the quayside.

The figure wearing the Homburg hat scrawled notes in pencil, noting not the beasts and the offloading, but the theatre of it all— the empire's display of power, arranged like a stage play for eager eyes.

Dickson's gaze never left the ship. The Biograph camera clicked rhythmically, capturing history in motion. This moment would not be lost.

The Zulu performers disembarked first. Showing off their beads, feathers, and spears they stood in stark contrast to the dull grey of the docks. They moved with quiet grace, the whispers of their journey trailing behind them.

Then, Basuto and Matabele warriors stepped forward. Their stories had travelled ahead of them—tales of strength, ferocity, and skill whispered from Cape Town to London. Now, as they set foot on English soil, the Biograph captured it all—the flash of spears, the glint of war shields, the silent endurance etched into their faces.

Among them was Pasha Liffey.

At five foot three, he did not tower over the others, yet something in the way he held himself drew the eye. This was his second crossing to England, but the thrill of arrival still coursed through him. The first time, he had come as a stable boy. Now, he was something else.

The crowd pressed closer. The Biograph lens followed the next phase of the spectacle—the horses, their coats gleaming, their hooves clattering against the gangplank. Then, zebras, shifting nervously, breath rising in the morning chill.

But the elephants stole the scene.

Handlers jabbed them forward with sharpened sticks, guiding them toward the waiting trains. Their great bodies swayed, trumpeting low, uneasy calls that trembled in the damp air.

The Biograph camera rolled as London's first glimpse of Africa flickered into history.

Near the quayside, the Zulu performers gathered in a loose group, their voices low. They spoke of the voyage, of what lay ahead, what they had left behind.

Then, Lobengula appeared.

He descended the gangplank with unhurried steps, dressed in tribal regalia. To some, he was Prince Lobengula, the self-proclaimed son of the Matabele king. To others, he was a man shadowed by stories and uncertain truths.

Frank Fillis moved swiftly to his side, murmuring a few words before steering him toward the group of Zulus.

Then, Fillis stepped forward.

He was the very picture of Victorian bravado—his top hat tilted just so, handlebar moustache bristling. He strode along the dock, a ringmaster in his element, gesturing sharply with his stick.

His voice rang out over the harbour noise.

At his command, the Zulu performers stirred, shifting restlessly—then, with sudden force, they broke into dance.

The Biograph camera whirred.

It captured every frame—each kick, each spear flashing in the light, each beat of the drummers' rhythm.

This was Indlamu. It was not for the crowd. It was for the ancestors.

A battle hymn that had echoed across the plains of Africa was now beating against the cold stone of Southampton—a dance of unbroken legacy, of untamed spirit, a story woven into movement.

The crowd watched in rapture.

The fog thickened, swallowing the edges of the dock, muffling the echoes of drums.

The Cape Town Rifles and Bechuanaland Police disembarked last. Their polished boots and gleaming rifles stood in sharp contrast to the warriors who had just danced, their presence a reminder of the Empire's reach.

A voice boomed through a megaphone, "all passengers, make your way to the train coaches! Boarding for London commences!"

Figures stirred to life, emerging like ghosts from the mist.

The voice followed, sharper, colder:

"A second train will take animal cargo. All beasts to be loaded."

Handlers moved swiftly, coaxing restless horses, moving lion cages, and ushering elephants.

Then, the disturbance began.

It started with Tommy.

The bull elephant reared suddenly, his thunderous roar splitting the dockside silence. The handlers scrambled, shouting orders, but fear had taken hold.

Tommy lunged, tusks tearing through a train carriage like paper.

Elephants charged down the platform, hooves pounding, leaving splintered wood and twisted metal in their wake.

Then, just as suddenly as it began, it was over.

Tommy stopped at the platform's edge. The others stilled behind him, their sides heaving.

A thick, uneasy silence settled over the wreckage.

Pasha stood, heart hammering.

The devastation was real enough, yet something older, more primal lingered in the air—a power that no ringmaster's stick could tame, no Empire could fully own.

It took hours to regain control.

The elephants, their fury spent, were led away. They would walk miles through the countryside, calming before rejoining the train at the next station.

As the last debris was cleared, Frank Fillis watched.

To most, this had been chaos, disaster.

To him, it was theatre.

This story—this legend of "Savage South Africa"—had just been written.

Beyond the wreckage, in the lingering mist, the journalist wearing the Homburg hat stood still.

His pencil had fallen silent, but his notebook held everything— every roar, every crash, every trembling shadow of something wild and untamed.

That night, as the newspaper presses clattered, London by the morning would know.

This was "Savage South Africa."

THE EMPIRE'S STAGE CALLS

At the docks, the train filled quickly—Matabele, Zulu, Basuto, Boers—strangers, yet bound by distant lands and the shared uncertainty of what lay ahead.

Pasha sat by the window, his gaze following the streaks of rain blurring the countryside into a shifting tapestry of greens and greys. The rhythmic clack of the train wheels against the tracks mirrored the slow detachment creeping over him. Each mile pulled him further from what he had known, carrying him into something undefined.

His time in England had given him much—a language, skills, the ability to move among those who would never fully accept him. Douglas Henry Fraser had brought him across the sea as a boy, a stable hand in a foreign world, yet no matter how much he learned, he had never shed the feeling of being an outsider. Even now, as the train rattled northward, that weight pressed against him, heavy as the clouds above.

Across from him, a man filled the narrow space—a giant, broad-shouldered beneath his traditional Zulu garb. The dark feathers in his headdress rose like spears. He was silent but not subdued. His presence didn't ask for attention.

Their eyes met. The man's gaze was steady, unreadable, but something flickered behind it—curiosity, maybe. Then, a slow, amused smile.

"Sawubona," he said, his voice deep, like distant thunder.

Pasha inclined his head. "Pasha."

The man nodded, the smile lingering. "Jacob Johnson," he said, his English crisp, deliberate. "They call me the Big Zulu."

Pasha lifted an eyebrow. "A Zulu by the name of Jacob Johnson?"

Jacob chuckled, a low, rolling sound. "A name for those bosses who need things to fit." His gaze drifted to the rain-streaked window. "It makes them more comfortable."

Pasha sat back, thoughtful. They were all playing parts—Zulu, Matabele, Swazi, Basuto—shaped into costumes and titles for an audience that saw only myth where there were men. It was theatre, and they were its players, paid in Queen's shillings.

"We're all playing parts, then," he said quietly.

Jacob's nod was slow. "They want warriors, not the truth."

The conversation faded into the steady rattle of the train. They sat silently, watching the landscape blur past the rain-etched windows, each lost in his own thoughts as the Empire pulled them deeper into its heart.

The first train hissed to a halt at Addison Road Station, swallowed by the mist of an early London morning. Heavy freight doors slid open, handlers stepping forward as the first creatures emerged.

The elephants came first, their massive feet pressing into the cobblestones with a low, resonant thud. Horses followed, their hooves clattering down the ramps, breath rising in sharp bursts.

Zebras, antelope, lions in their iron-barred cages. Golden eyes flicked through the fog, scanning this new, unfamiliar world.

The streets of Kensington had never seen anything like it.

The procession began, winding its way through Addison Road and onto Warwick Road. The animals moved nervously, shifting shadows against the wet streets. The elephants swayed, their handlers murmuring soft commands, prodding when needed.

House windows opened, doors edged ajar. Londoners watched.

Children clung to their mother's skirts, eyes round with awe. Men stood still, hats tipped, hands buried in pockets. Women drew shawls closer, hesitant, uncertain whether to edge forward or retreat. Low whispers rippled through the fog. The soft creak of the lions' cages. The muffled thud of hooves on wet stone.

As the fog thinned, the city took form again—streets taking shape, signs readable, the imposing shadow of Earl's Court ahead.

For those watching, this was more than a parade of animals—it was a collision of worlds. The wild had been harnessed, dragged from distant lands and paraded through their streets. For a fleeting moment, something raw and untamed pressed against the edges of their orderly city, leaving behind an unease that would linger long after the procession passed.

Fifty-four minutes later, the second train arrived at West Brompton.

Steam hissed from the locomotive's stack, unravelling in ghostly ribbons, while thick smoke curled upward, carrying the sharp scent of coal dust. The train ground to a halt beneath the iron lattice of the station, its heat lingering in the cool air. The doors swung open, and the performers of *Savage South Africa* stepped onto the platform.

Pasha adjusted his coat against the cold drizzle. Beside him, Jacob tugged his headdress tighter. No one spoke. The air was thick with something unspoken tension.

There was no turning back now.

The extravaganza was ready to consume them, to shape them into something only Fillis would understand. *Savage South Africa* was more than a spectacle—it was a machine, relentless in its hunger for myth and fantasy. It would take their names, their histories, and their identities, shifting them into something palatable, something that fit neatly within the Empire's idea of the exotic and the conquered. They had stepped onto the platform as men, warriors, storytellers, and survivors. But by the time the show began, they would become something else entirely—characters in a grand illusion, their realities swallowed by the demands of entertainment.

Rain fell in a fine, persistent drizzle, turning the cobblestones slick beneath their boots. The city watched.

Then Earl's Court loomed before them.

The iron and stone façade loomed against the grey sky, its vast arches stark against the early afternoon light. Within those walls, the world of Savage South Africa had already been constructed, waiting for its players to step into place.

For the men of Basutoland, Zululand, Matabeleland, this would be home for months. Here, they would be seen but never known, observed but never understood.

Pasha felt something tighten in his chest.

He knew they would play their parts, but even in performance, there was power.

He glanced at Jacob, whose towering frame stood at the threshold. There was fire in the man's eyes, something untamed. He was not broken.

With a deep breath, Pasha stepped forward into the shadowed world of Earl's Court.

The sounds of London faded behind him.

INK AND SHADOWS

R ead all about it! Read all about it! Wild beasts and warriors have arrived. They are here!" The newspaper boy's cry pierced the clamour of Fleet Street, his voice barely reaching above the thundering carriages and bustling crowd. He stood outside the Wine Office Court, waving his stack of newspapers as if his life depended on it. His keen eyes darted between the hurried passersby, catching their attention with an audacious gleam.

A journalist in a well-worn Homburg hat paused at the boy's cry. He sent a copper coin spinning through the air with a deft flick. The boy's fingers snatched it mid-flight, a practised motion, and he handed over a fresh copy of "The Times". The journalist tucked the paper into his coat pocket and moved down the narrow alley toward "Ye Olde Cheshire Cheese", the venerable pub nestled inconspicuously at the end of Wine Office Court.

As he ducked beneath the low archway marking the entrance, he stepped into a place soaked in history. The scent of smoke and aged wood enveloped him, mingling with the faint tang of stale ale. Around him, shadows of past patrons lingered—a reminder of the many great minds who had taken refuge here over the centuries. His eyes wandered to the old wooden tables and benches where, not too many years ago, figures like G.K. Chesterton and W.T. Stead might have held court, weaving tales as thick as the smoke that clung to the rafters. Even Rudyard Kipling had passed through, exchanging stories with poets and pressmen as he pondered the Empire that loomed large beyond the walls.

The man wearing the Homburg hat offered the landlord a brief nod before navigating the dim staircase to his cramped office above, an oasis of sorts amidst the thrumming life of Fleet Street. His office was a monument to his work, scattered with stacks of paper, clippings, and scrawled notes detailing a thousand unfinished stories. With a huff, he dropped his hat onto the cluttered desk. Opening the freshly printed paper with a flick of his wrist, anticipation flickering in his eyes, his face fell as he scanned the pages. His story wasn't there. The "Times" had yet to run it, his words swallowed up by the day's headlines.

With a resigned sigh, he tossed the paper onto his desk. His ever-diligent secretary had been through earlier, leaving a neat stack of clippings carefully organised on the desk. They were all there: sensationalised accounts from the Wishaw Press including The Church Weekly, twisting his intended narrative into one that veered dangerously close to caricature.

The Wishaw Press headline glared back at him: "Savage South Africa" Lands in England! His eyes skimmed over the text, teeth clenched as he read: "Some very remarkable 'alien immigrants' effected a landing on our shores the other day. Several of them testified their delight at reaching this 'land of the brave and the free' by executing a saraband at the quay at Southampton…"

A clipping from The Church Weekly continued the same mocking tone:

"With the human visitors, who number a couple of hundred, come many animals of various kinds, including about 80 horses and ponies, and some elephants, lions, monkeys, and other creatures, all strange and wonderful..."

He sighed, his fingers tightening around the edges of the article. Even among his colleagues, the performers—Zulu, Basuto, Swazi, and Matabele—seemed reduced to spectacles, their humanity washed away by the ink of sensationalism.

Setting down the paper clippings, he stepped down the staircase, the pub's familiar sounds and steady warmth comforting him. He slid onto a well-worn stool at the bar, nodding to the barman, who poured a finger of whisky, the amber liquid catching the dim light. This was a pub where Jerome K. Jerome had once mused on the absurdities of life, where Alfred Harmsworth— Lord Northcliffe—might have bellowed about the latest newsprint sensation. In the heart of Fleet Street's history, the man with the Homburg hat felt both humbled and frustrated, acutely aware of the legacy pressing in around him.

He took a slow sip, the warmth settling in his chest, bracing him for tomorrow. Around him, the pub hummed with voices—some mocking, some wise, some slipping unnoticed into the smoky air. He knew that despite the spectacle his story had become, twisted into something fit for a carnival, the truth still remained. It might not grace the pages of *The Times* today, but he would make sure it did soon.

As he drained the glass, his gaze drifted to the dim corners of the room, where the light wavered against the walls, shadows shifting like silent witnesses to history's steady march.

THE ETHICS OF EMPIRE

April 28, 1899

The "Savage South Africa" show at Earl's Court drew hundreds of thousands—some claimed over a million—all lured by its spectacle. Zulu warriors, roaring lions, elephants lumbering beneath the gaslights—London watched, enthralled, awed by its own Empire.

The Daily Mail and Illustrated London News hailed the exhibition as a pageant of Empire, proof of British dominion. But in the quieter columns of the Daily News and Pall Mall Gazette, unease crept in. Were these warriors or exhibits? Men or curiosities?

Rumours spread that many of the Zulu men and women had been brought to London under false pretences, misled with promises of work in the Kimberley mines, only to find themselves paraded in London's cold, crowded streets. For many the exhibition was nothing more than a display of conquest wrapped in pomp, with an uneasy hint of exploitation shadowing exotic pageantry.

Disquiet turned to debate. In the House of Commons, voices rose—not in awe, but unease. Across the chamber, men argued not over warriors or lions but over the line between spectacle and shame.

In every newspaper headline, in every discussion, the shine of the show dimmed in the eyes of a restless few who saw through the spectacle to the uncomfortable truths beneath.

From the press box in the House of Commons, a journalist leaned forward, his pencil poised as he scanned the chamber. Below, the figures of Parliament murmured amongst themselves, seated on leather benches that glowed softly under the chamber's gaslights. The words of Sir Robert Reid, a Scottish Liberal MP and critic of imperial exploitation, resonated through the chamber. "Mr. Speaker," Reid began, cutting through the ambient rustle of shifting papers and murmured conversations. "I beg to ask the Secretary of State for the Colonies if he is aware that the Governments of the Cape, Natal, the Orange Free State, and the Transvaal have expressed their disapproval of the introduction of native men and women into this country for the so-called 'Savage South Africa' exhibition."

The journalist's pencil scratched rapidly, capturing every word. His shorthand strokes were quick and efficient, but something about the proceedings held his focus, urging him to listen more closely. Reid continued, his tone pressing further, challenging the government's stance on the ethics of such an exhibition.

A glance at the other members of the press box revealed a similar quiet absorption. Each journalist leaned over his notebook, noting every nuance, understanding that this story would stretch far beyond the walls of Parliament.

Joseph Chamberlain rose, his expression neutral and practised. But the journalist saw it—the slight shift of his stance, the fingers pressing against the lectern, as though steadying himself against the weight of his own words. "The answer, Sir Robert, is yes," Chamberlain began, his voice carrying a faint, almost regretful resonance. "Like the High Commissioner, the Cape and

Natal governments have expressed disapproval." He paused, a flicker of discomfort shadowing his brow. "I must also add that I concur with their opinions."

A murmur rippled through the chamber, the quiet agreement stirring in waves. Some MPs nodded, brows furrowed as they grappled with the ethics of an exhibition that blurred the lines between entertainment and exploitation. But others, scattered across the chamber, sat with scepticism etched on their faces as if such concerns were an indulgence unworthy of Parliament's time.

Reid, however, was not finished. He pressed on, unwilling to let the matter rest. "Might the High Commissioner and Cape Government correspondence be laid before the House?"

Chamberlain's reply was curt, his grip tightening momentarily on the lectern. "I do not propose to do so, but the honourable member may view the correspondence at the Colonial Office if he desires."

The journalist paused writing in his notebook. In Chamberlain's words, he sensed a resignation, a tension that hinted at more than just Parliamentary decorum. Here was a man caught in the web of politics, his reluctance evident. Still, his role forced him to uphold the machinery of the Empire.

From the back benches, another voice rang out, cutting sharply through the low hum. "Mr. Speaker, is it not true," came the question from T. Bayley, MP for Chesterfield, "that fifty Zulu men were led to believe they would be employed in the

Kimberley Mines, only to find themselves shipped here to be exhibited like animals in this show?"

A renewed unease swept the room, and the journalist shifted in the press box. This was more than a scandal—it was a point of moral reckoning. Bayley's voice, rising with each phrase, echoed with a biting critique. "Native women, too, were procured through advertisements, promising positions that appear dubious at best. Can the Secretary of State explain why the Governments of the British Colonies and the Dutch States in South Africa protested this exportation on the grounds of morality and good governance, yet the exhibition continues?"

Chamberlain's mask slipped momentarily, a flicker of irritation crossing his face. "I am aware of the concerns the Cape and Natal governments raised," he began, calm and controlled. "However, Her Majesty's Government has no power to compel the return of these natives. I can only express my regret and disapproval of their introduction."

The journalist's fingers tightened on his pencil. Regret and disapproval—words that rang hollow here, cloaked in the softened phrasing of bureaucracy. "We regret the government's hands were tied", Chamberlain said, leaving the journalist to wonder just how far those constraints stretched and how much was choice masked as policy.

Reid's voice cut through once more, this time sharper, his patience waning. "Regret, Mr. Chamberlain? Regret is not enough. This is not just a matter of exhibition or entertainment. This is a moral issue. We have a duty to these people, a responsibility that extends beyond the boundaries of this House and into the colonies we claim to govern."

A hush fell over the chamber, Reid's words leaving a palpable weight. At that moment, as the moral weight of the argument settled on the room, even the journalist felt the sting of that responsibility—a sense that Parliament had taken a step beyond mere debate into territory where ethics could no longer be ignored.

Chamberlain, unyielding, squared his shoulders. "I had not observed that the show was to be opened by the Duke of Cambridge," his voice firm, "but I now propose to communicate with His Royal Highness on the matter."

The Duke's name hung in the air, adding an unexpected gravity to the debate. Even the journalist felt a quiet ripple of surprise; this show, it seemed, was more than a spectacle—it was an affair of the Empire.

From his seat in the press box, the journalist tucked his notebook away, the echoes of Reid's words still ringing in his ears. The session had ended, but the real battle outside these polished halls was beginning.

Soon, his story would be ink on paper.

BETWEEN TWO WORLDS

The air was sharp with the late April cold as the performers from "Savage South Africa" made their way to Earl's Court to claim their village—if it could be called that. The British had built the "Kraal" from sketches and distant memories, a lifeless replica meant for viewing, not living. As the men and women arrived from their hotel rooms, the sight met them like an exhibit waiting for its glass case.

As they approached the "Kraal", the Zulu, Swazi, Basuto, and Matabele performers walked through the half-formed maze with careful eyes. Their laughter was soft but unmistakable, a fragile sound amidst the sharp chill in the air. Pasha let a grin slip as he gazed down at the polished wooden floors—an overly ambitious attempt at comfort by city men who had little understanding of what a true "Kraal" required. The scent of fresh wood and varnish hung heavy, almost clinical, compared to the home's rich, earthy aroma. "A "Kraal" fit for a man who dislikes the smell of Kraals, Pasha mused, irony threading through his thoughts.

Despite its flaws, this would be their home for as long as the spring and autumn would allow. It was clear they needed to make it their own. The British builders had hammered in posts and lashed reeds to the walls, but the "Kraal" lacked the warmth of home, the details that transformed it into a sanctuary.

Determined, they set to work. Reeds, woven mats, skins—each piece laid down with practised hands, each touch a quiet rebellion. They could not change the wooden floors, but they layered warmth where cold had been built, stitching memory into every corner. It would never be home, but it would be theirs.

As Pasha worked, something unsettled him—a feeling he couldn't name, as foreign as the London cold seeping through his clothes. They were building a home that wasn't a home. The words 'home' and 'display' blurred together, indistinct. Perhaps this was his world now—caught between places, always more seen than known.

Pasha and his fellow performers transformed the hastily built huts in the "Kraal" into a semblance of their own culture. They were not merely completing a set but reclaiming a piece of their identity. While this "Kraal" had been constructed to mimic Africa, it was up to them to imbue it with life. Each woven mat, every familiar object they laid down, became an act of defiance—a reminder that even beneath the London fog, they would maintain their sense of belonging.

Beyond the Kraal, London was waiting.

The newspapers had done their work, filling columns with bold promises—"Savage South Africa! The Greatest Ethnological Exhibition of Our Time!" The city hummed with curiosity, anticipation rippling through drawing rooms and docklands. In grand townhouses, gentlemen circled dates in their diaries, discussing empire and spectacle over brandy and cigars. Military men, fresh from postings in distant colonies, speculated whether the Zulus would be as formidable in a performance as they had been in war.

In quieter streets, the expectation took a different shape. Factory workers passed handbills between calloused fingers, squinting at illustrations of warriors and wild animals. Chimney sweeps and errand boys dreamed of slipping past the gates for a glimpse of something untamed, something beyond the soot and stone of London life. In dimly lit parlours, mothers recounted tales of Africa to wide-eyed children, their stories spun from scraps of newspaper reports and the myths of the Empire.

The show had not yet begun, but London had already decided what it would see.

And within the Kraal, the performers waited too—but not with the same ease. The fences were up, the earth packed beneath their feet, the illusion nearly complete. Already, they could feel the weight of watching eyes that were not yet there.

And as Pasha stood amidst the remnants of his culture, he felt the weight of expectation settle upon him. Soon, he would step into the limelight, embodying the fantasies of an audience that would never fully understand the richness of the lives behind the performance. Yet, for now, as he helped rebuild their village, he felt the flicker of hope that, despite it all, they could carve out a space that felt like home, if only for a moment.

SHADOW OF THE SPECTACLE

London, 8 May 1899

The second week of May. The sun fractured across the streets of West Kensington as the city braced for another night of "Savage South Africa."

It was a Wednesday evening, and at Earl's Court, "Savage South Africa" was about to captivate the imagination of Londoners— thousands of them. People came from all directions—through Warwick Road, along Old Brompton Road, and winding their way down Empress Place— surging towards the towering gates, eager to witness the empire's might displayed in vivid spectacle.

The flags above the Earls Court entrance flapped lazily, muted by the evening mist. Yet their symbolism remained unmistakable. Britain ruled. Britain conquered. And tonight, the people of London would witness the retelling of conquest, draped in the grand spectacle of exotic warriors and British heroes locked in a dramatic, timeless battle.

Men in starched collars and top hats jostled beside chimney sweeps, their faces smudged with soot. Women in white gloves clutched silk purses, their breaths ghosting in the cool air. Children bounced on their toes, pulled along by the tide of bodies, their excitement bright and unfiltered.

The crowd was pulled not only to the allure of grand displays of colonial might but also to the undercurrent of danger and mystery, the promise of wild, untamed Africa brought to heel beneath the iron hand of British rule.

The performers—Zulus, Swazis, Matabele, Basuto, Boers and the Empire Police and Military —had crossed the oceans to play their part in this grand theatre, their presence both exotic and unsettling to the Victorian crowd.

The crowd settled in the arena seats. There was the odd cough and, eventually, a hush. For many, this was their first glimpse of Africa, or what they believed Africa to be: fierce, primal, and yet subdued for the glory of the Empire.

Against the backdrop of a painted African scrubland, a mail coach creaked forward, its wheels groaning in protest, pulled by nervous mules. The men aboard the stagecoach gripped their rifles.

They came out of the shadows—hundreds of warriors, moving with deadly precision, their spears and rifles glinting under a distant, flickering fire. They were silent, shadows on the wind, sweeping across the showground like phantoms summoned from the depths of Africa.

Gunfire shattered the night. Muzzle flashes carved brief, jagged light into the darkness, revealing the defenders' wild, desperate faces. They fired into the charging warriors.

The warriors charged the mail coach. Their war cries, mixed with drumbeats pounding like the roll of thunder, filled the stadium. Their spears—flashing under the arena's gas and arc lights— rained down on the coach. The ground trembled as the warriors surged forward, their ranks a tide of bodies, wild and unstoppable.

The journalist with the Homburg hat sat in the crowd. Unlike the crowd, whose gazes were locked on the action, his attention flickered between the performance and the audience. He captured the responses of those around him—how their faces tightened in awe, their hands clenched the wooden armrests, their breath caught in their throats.

Rifle fire and cries filled the arena as the warriors descended upon the coach. Their charge shook the ground. The journalist's pencil danced across the page, capturing the crowd's reactions.

The coach lurched, the mules rearing as the wheels spun helplessly in the dirt. The warriors closed in on the coach, and the men aboard fled into the bush.

The warriors, emboldened by their victory, turned toward the flickering lights of the homestead, their cries now a deafening roar. Spears raised high, they swept forward, and they were upon the homestead in moments. Spears crashed through wooden walls, tearing the tiny houses apart. The settlers fought with a grim, hopeless fury, their rifles firing wildly as the walls caved around them.

The homestead was now alight - flames reaching the sky.

Amid the chaos, a single woman broke free, her revolver held tightly in her hand; she ran for the cliff. The warriors pursued, spears flashing in the firelight, but she did not stop. Reaching the cliff's edge, she turned, firing one last shot into the night before leaping off the cliff and vanishing into the black waters below, leaving nothing but ripples in her wake.

The scene in the arena was chaotic, yet it was just part of the story for the journalist. His pencil paused as the woman leapt from the cliff's edge. He noted the audience's collective breath, held for a moment too long, and how the roar of the warriors carried a different weight now. He was observing every ripple of the unfolding drama.

And then, from the smoke and flames surrounding the homestead, the Matabele King emerged.

Tall, broad-shouldered, and draped in the skin of a great lion, the King strode forward with the weight of history behind him.

The light from the flames caught Lobengula's body, casting him in an otherworldly glow. Warriors parted for him as he advanced, their chants and war cries falling silent in reverence. He raised his spear, signalling his warriors to hold.

A bugle sounded - and a formation of British soldiers appeared - a party to avenge the fallen of the coach and the homestead.

The soldiers dismounted, laid their capes on the ground, and tethered their horses. They formed a defensive square—a last-stand square. The heavy and deadly Maxim machine guns were wheeled into place.

The King hurled his spear toward the British line. It struck the ground —a signal, not of peace but of finality, a command for his warriors to strike the killing blow.

The warriors surged forward.

The bugle called again, urging the British assembly to hold. The warriors came, a tide of bodies, war cries rising into a crescendo that shook the earth.

The Maxim chattered, spitting fire and bullets into the charging horde. Warriors fell.

The British soldiers braced themselves, rifles raised as clubs, knowing their bullets were spent. But it was hopeless. The warriors crashed into them with the force of a thunderstorm, bodies colliding in a desperate struggle. The sound of metal on metal, wood on flesh, filled the air as the British fought for their lives, swinging their rifles wildly.

But it was not enough.

One by one, the British soldiers fell, their bodies crumpling to the ground. Once the pride of the empire's military, the Maxim guns lay silent—useless in the face of such overwhelming numbers. Their operators, the last to fall, died with their hands still gripping their weapons, defiant even in death.

The British line was obliterated. There was no victory to be found here—only the quiet, inevitable end of men outmatched and outnumbered.

The Matabele warriors stood victorious, their spears raised high as they surveyed the battlefield. The bodies of the British soldiers lay strewn across the dirt.

As the re-enactment faded, the journalist leaned back slightly, his hand moving again. He noted the way the British soldiers fell with their rifles still in hand, their last moments captured under the artificial lights of Earl's Court. The applause from the crowd did not move him; he remained silent and pensive before rising from his seat. Gripping a Goerz Anschütz camera, a photographer glanced at the journalist. They knew they had captured history.

As the performance drew to its triumphant close, Pasha stood among the ranks of the Matabele warriors, his spear lowered, his chest heaving from the exertion. The crowd's cheers roared around him, a wall of sound that seemed to press in from all sides. Yet, for all its energy, it felt hollow. The cheers weren't for him—not for the Basuto boy who had crossed oceans—but for the lie they had dressed him in.

He shifted his grip on the spear, its smooth, polished wood foreign in his hands—a weapon meant for warriors, not for someone who had spent most of his life tending horses. Its absurdity struck him again, as it always did during these performances. A Basuto pretending to be a Matabele warrior, roaring battle cries that he did not understand, charging into an artificial war beneath the blinding lights of Earl's Court.

As the applause swelled and the chants of the other performers echoed around him, Pasha felt a flicker of something he could not quite name. Pride? Shame? A strange mixture of both, perhaps, twisted with exhaustion and the weight of the expectations placed upon him.

The cheers grew louder, reverberating through the arena. He glanced toward the audience for a moment—rows upon rows of pale faces, their eyes wide with awe. Did they see him? He was not sure if he wanted them to.

The journalist vanished into the night, but the spectacle clung to him—the cheers, the dust, the uneasy triumph of it all. The questions it raised would spill onto the page, yet he already knew that some truths would remain elusive, lost beneath the crowd's roar.

FRAGMENTS OF DISORDER

May 18, 1899

His Homburg hat rested on the back of his wooden chair, its brim sloping downwards as if pondering the mood unfolding in the dimly lit office.

Outside, rain began to tap softly against the window, creating a gentle rhythm that barely disturbed the heavy silence within.

The journalist hunched over his desk.

Before him lay a scattered collection of newspapers - headlines, ink-stained and wrinkled at the edges, each more unsettling than the last.

He had returned from "Savage South Africa" at Earl's Court only an hour ago. His coat hung on the hook by the door, damp from the London mist that strangled the city.

He settled into the task before him in the quiet of his office, far from the spectacle of the exhibition grounds. The stories, the whispers, the contradictions—*Savage South Africa* was spiralling into something far beyond its intended spectacle.

He slid open the drawer and took out a bottle of whisky, its weight familiar in his hand. Pouring a generous measure, he lifted the glass and took a sip, letting the amber liquid coat his tongue before swallowing—the burn grounding him. The desk before him was a battlefield of ink and paper—cuttings, telegrams, notes—each one a fragment of the growing storm. He sifted through them with steady hands, scanning bold headlines, tracing hurried scribbles in the margins, piecing together a picture that refused to sit still.

Some reports praised the grandeur, the Empire's might on full display. Others hinted at something more unsettling—unease behind the painted faces, tension beneath the applause. The *Hull Evening News* took a brash tone, while *The Times* measured its words more carefully. He clipped another article, smoothing it flat, adding it to the growing stack he would soon send across the ocean.

Outside, the city hummed with its usual distractions, but in this office, he was deep in the undercurrent, searching for what lay beneath the spectacle. This was not just a performance—it was something else.

From the Hull Evening News: *"Savage South Africa is upholding its name. One of the Cape boys at Earl's Court, primed with beer and armed with an iron bar, has been running amok. His antics struck terror to the heart of the feminine portion of the community."*

Next, he selected Reynold's Newspaper, the ink smudging slightly as his thumb traced the bold typeface. He whispered, *"Disorder at Earl's Court, tensions among the participants. The wild show, once a dazzling spectacle, now faces growing scrutiny from the public and officials alike."*

He leaned back, his chair creaking in protest, eyes narrowing at the mess of headlines. At first, "Savage South Africa" had been all glitter and pomp—a spectacle for the Empire's hungry eyes. Zulu dancers, Matabele warriors, lions in their iron cages. But now, the sheen was fading. The cracks were no longer cracks; they were fractures, widening with every performance. The performers, once proud and composed, were being worn down, stripped bare by the relentless glare of performance. And the drink flowed too freely, numbing the pain of displacement, of being paraded like curiosities in front of a gawking, restless crowd.

The journalist's fingers traced the edges of the newsprint, his pencil resting idly on the desk. He felt it in his bones—the slow, inevitable spiral. The show wasn't just unravelling but collapsing under its contradictions.

From the Sunday Dispatch: *"One of the Cape boys, primed with liquor, armed with a fighting stick struck terror in the heart of the neighbourhood... fined and shipped back to his native land."*

The rhythm was all too familiar—booze-fuelled fights, accusations, fines, and then quiet deportations. The men, who had once walked with dignity, were being reduced to mere shadows, pushed to the edge by the spectacle and exploitation. And yet, the show went on.

From The Times: *"The savage exhibition, once a spectacle of great interest, is now under scrutiny. Complaints have surfaced regarding disorderly behaviour, drunkenness, and public indecency among the participants."*

He rubbed his eyes, exhaustion creeping in as the rain outside intensified, pattering against the window. He took another sip of whisky, this time slower, savouring the burn as it wound its way down, but it did little to clear the fog in his mind. How did it come to this? He wondered. A few short weeks ago, they had marched into London with their heads held high.

From the Fulham and Hammersmith Chronicle: *"The aborigines of "Savage South Africa" are restless, their behaviour increasingly unruly… incidents of disorderly conduct, particularly among the Cape boys, have led to several fines and deportations."*

The folder was becoming thick now, bursting with stories from nationwide. His hand had marked it neat and deliberate, *'To Vere Stent.'* These clippings would take three or more weeks to reach Cape Town by ship, but he knew they were worth the wait. Stent received daily feeds from Reuters—concise, polished, and direct. But these cuttings, though late, brought another dimension. They carried the weight of varied voices, of different angles, and most importantly, they were proof that the grand spectacle was crumbling, even in the eyes of the press.

As he carefully placed the last clipping in the folder, his thoughts drifted back to Cape Town, where he had first met Stent. Their paths had crossed during the colonial administration's turmoil, working as young journalists eager to uncover the truth beneath the surface. Stent, always insightful and sharp, had become an editor. At the same time, he had remained a correspondent, feeding stories from the heart of the Empire. They had exchanged letters ever since, each recognising the other's dedication to exposing the cracks in the grand facade. With "Savage South Africa" spiralling out of control, these clippings were more than just reports—they were a testament to the crumbling illusions they both sought to illuminate. The rain outside continued, steady, and rhythmic, as he stood and crossed the room to the window. Tomorrow, the papers would carry more stories—fights, fines, deportations. The show would go on. But he knew, deep down, it was already over.

Forgotten, his pencil rolled off the edge of the desk, clattering softly to the floor.

CLASH OF STICKS AND SPIRITS

Late June 1899

The air at The Kraal was thick with dark, simmering tension—an uneasy pulse beneath the polished spectacle of *Savage South Africa*. What had once been a shared novelty had fractured into rivalries, cliques, and resentments. The show continued under London's bright lights, but beneath that surface, a storm was brewing.

Between the Swazi and Basuto huts, two figures squared up—each brandishing a fighting stick. One was a lean Basuto, the other a towering Swazi. The argument, stoked by drink, had begun over territorial wars that had raged decades earlier when King Moshoeshoe I ruled. Now, in a foreign land, old conflicts demanded resolution.

There was only one way to settle it.

A stick fight.

In the fire-lit ring, surrounded by murmurs and shifting shadows, this was no staged battle. It was tradition—a contest of will and endurance, a test as old as the lands they had left behind. The London crowd watched, breathless, caught between fascination and unease.

The Basuto struck first, his stick a blur in the firelight, fast as a boomslang. The Swazi absorbed each attack, meeting speed with brute force, his counterstrikes deliberate, unyielding. The sound of wood cracking against wood filled the air.

Gasps rippled through the onlookers as blows landed. A dance of skill and fury.

The Basuto lunged, his strike swift and final—but his foot caught on uneven ground. That brief misstep cost him. The Swazi's stick came down hard, cracking against his face. Pain flared as his lip split open, blood spraying onto the dirt.

The Basuto dropped to his knees, his stick falling. In surrender, he cast it aside.

The moment shattered as Boer guards stormed in, rough hands dragging the fighters toward the animal cages at the edge of the camp. A murmur ran through the crowd—half intrigued, half repelled. The Londoners had come for a spectacle, but this felt different.

Texas Jack forced his way through, his voice once a force of command, now struggling for authority.

"Enough!" he bellowed, but no one flinched.

The performers no longer feared him. The months in London—the alcohol, the gambling, the late-night fights—had eroded the fragile order. Discipline had unravelled.

Behind Texas Jack, Frank Fillis clenched his jaw, already framing a story for the press. The journalists had arrived, scribbling furiously, their sharp eyes catching every detail—the bloodied earth, the men thrown into iron cages, the flickering uncertainty in Fillis' expression.

"Just a little dust-up," Fillis forced a grin. "No police required." They didn't believe him.

One journalist, his long dark coat trailing in the dirt, arrived as the crowd peeled away. He hadn't seen the fight, only the aftermath. Blood. Silence. The weight of something shifting beneath the surface.

His pencil moved quickly, relentlessly, capturing not the fight but the unravelling edges of the camp: the Boer guards, watching with quiet disdain; Texas Jack, shouting orders no one listened to; and the flicker of uncertainty in Fillis' voice.

The Kraal was no longer just a show. It was a tinderbox.

Inside the cage, the Basuto pressed a rag to his bleeding lip, the taste of iron thick on his tongue. He felt the Boer guards' eyes on him, their silent judgement heavier than the bars.

The Swazi, still streaked with his own blood, caught his gaze and nodded—a silent recognition.

There was no victory here.

At dawn, the cages were unlocked. The Basuto staggered back to his hut, exhaustion pressing into his bones. The fight was over, but something larger had begun.

The show officials convened a brief inquiry—a farce of justice. Decisions had already been made.

On June 24, fourteen men were pulled from the camp, names read aloud, their fate sealed. They were marched to the docks, booked onto the Union Steamship liner Gaika.

No trial. No explanation. Just deportation.

Pasha watched from a distance, counting them. He knew more would follow.

A MARRIAGE
AGAINST THE GRAIN

B ehind the grand façade of Earl's Court, beneath the dazzling veneer of spectacle, a storm gathered in whispers and knowing glances, its edges sharp with scandal. It was June 1899, and the first rays of the solstice spread along London's pavements, stretching shadows and illuminating the restless city. *Savage South Africa* continued to lure the curious and the enthralled, drawing spectators from every district, their fascination with Zulu warriors, caged lions, and exotic displays unbroken. Yet, beyond the performances, beyond the carefully orchestrated pageantry, it was the quiet murmurs of something altogether more disruptive that truly held London in its grasp—a scandal that revolved around Lobengula, the towering Matabele warrior who claimed lineage to a king, and his defiant, passionate affair with Florence Kate Jewell, known simply as Kitty.

At his desk, the journalist surveyed the scattered newspaper clippings before him; their edges curled from repeated handling, the ink smudged against his fingertips as he turned over another sensational account of the affair. With all their hyperbole and feigned outrage, these stories had gripped the city in a way that even *Savage South Africa* had failed to do, stirring tempers in private parlours as much as in the alehouses of the East End.

He had written of many scandals before and had documented the missteps of aristocrats and the follies of men who had flown too close to the fire of their own ambition, but this was different. This was not simply a story of love, nor was it just rebellion—it was a confrontation between race and Empire, an act of defiance against an unspoken order that had long dictated the boundaries between people, the strictures of class, and the unyielding rules of who was permitted to love whom. He knew, as he scanned the headlines, that the true story was buried beneath the ink, submerged beneath the spectacle of it all.

Their tale had not begun here, in London, nor beneath the dim glow of gaslights in the streets that twisted through the heart of the Empire. It had begun long before, on the sun-scorched plains of South Africa, where Kitty had first crossed paths with Lobengula, in a place far removed from the drawing rooms of Mayfair or the cobbled streets of Kensington. It was in Bloemfontein, during one of her father's ventures into the world of mining and business, that she had first encountered him. Her father, a Welshman who had carved a fortune out of the earth's depths, had made his wealth amidst the land's diamond fields and shifting fortunes. But while her family concerned themselves with commerce and empire-building, Kitty had been captivated by something else entirely.

It was beneath the vast African sky that she had first seen him, a man unlike any she had known before, a figure who seemed to move through the world with quiet certainty; his presence imbued with something intangible yet undeniable. Even then, he had possessed an air of quiet authority, a bearing that set him apart, whether by birthright or by the sheer force of his being. The question of whether it was blood or spirit that made him regal had never truly been answered, yet Kitty had felt it nonetheless—something raw and unspoken, an attraction that had smouldered beneath the surface for years before it found its inevitable reckoning here, in the very heart of the Empire.

The journalist's pencil moved steadily over the page as he considered the weight of Lobengula's presence, the way in which he had become an enigma not only to Kitty but to the British public at large. He was a mystery, a man who had stepped out of the pages of the Empire's stories, fashioned into something both admired and feared. But the question lingered still—was he truly of royal blood, the son of King Lobengula, or had he simply become a construct of the Empire's insatiable hunger for spectacle, a figure onto whom they could project their own imaginings of power and primitivism? Even Pasha, watching from the periphery of it all, could never quite decide.

Lifting his glass, the journalist took a slow sip of whisky, letting its warmth settle within him as he turned his attention to another clipping, its bold print blaring the scandal in garish type. At first, the affair had been no more than a whisper, a thing noticed in passing by those accustomed to keeping their eyes open and their voices hushed. But the press, relentless in its pursuit of controversy, had seized upon it with enthusiasm. The *Evening News* had been the first to print it, branding Kitty reckless, reckless enough to entangle herself with the so-called savage prince, a man the British public had once been content to admire from a distance but whose presence now unnerved them when brought too close to their own world. The *Daily Mail* followed swiftly, the language of its coverage more pointed, laced with the suggestion of moral decay, of a warning against the dangers such a union posed to the fabric of British society.

Kitty, once regarded as nothing more than a woman of means, had become a figure of both fascination and condemnation, a subject of fevered debate and derision. Where once Lobengula had been celebrated as an exotic curiosity, a warrior upon the stage, now he found himself scrutinised with suspicion, the once-thrilling mystery of his presence now transformed into something to be feared. The journalist, reading between the lines of every article, recognised the shift. The public had adored the performance, the grand theatre of it all, but the moment the spectacle ceased to be contained within the safe parameters of their expectation, their admiration had turned to unease.

Yet, despite the mounting storm, despite the escalating headlines and the whispers in drawing rooms and taverns alike, Kitty and Lobengula's love endured.

As the summer deepened, so too did the controversy surrounding them, their names passing from the lips of aristocrats who gossiped over tea to the factory workers who spoke of them over tankards of ale. Their affair was no longer just about two people—it had become a symbol of something far larger than either of them, a challenge to the rigid structures that governed Empire, race, and belonging.

Even as they fought to defy the forces that sought to drive them apart, the weight of those forces pressed heavily upon them. When they sought to marry in the Church of England, their request was met with outright refusal, the doors of every parish they approached closing firmly in their faces. Undeterred, they searched for another path, seeking out registry offices where the rigidity of the Church's decrees might be bypassed.

And so, in a small, unremarkable office, far removed from the grand halls of London's elite, with no flowers, no pews lined with guests, and no clergy to bless their union, they spoke the words that bound them together in law, if not in the eyes of a world that refused to acknowledge them.

As they stepped out into the fading light of day, their hands entwined, they understood, without needing to say it aloud, that what they had done extended beyond romance or rebellion.

Nearby, the journalist lingered, his pencil still poised above the worn pages of his notebook, watching as they moved together through the streets of a city that would never truly accept them. He had spent enough time within the confines of Earl's Court to know that this was no fleeting affair, no mere scandal to be consumed and discarded by the public. This was something far greater—an act of quiet defiance against the expectations of an empire that sought to dictate the boundaries of love and identity.

In the shadows, Pasha watched as well, understanding the precariousness of it all, knowing that the world they had dared to challenge was one that would not hesitate to strike back. Yet, even amidst the gathering storm, he saw in them something impervious to the weight of law, of prejudice, and of the Empire —a force that no decree or condemnation could truly erase.

UNDER THE WEIGHT OF THE LENS

The murmur of voices faded as Joseph Rosenthal stepped forward, his wiry frame taut with energy. His sharp voice cut across the arena, an accent difficult to place—shaped by many borders yet belonging to none.

"Gentlemen, meet The Beast."

A hush followed. Before him loomed the Biograph camera—wood, gears, and ambition fused into one mechanical colossus. The weight of it—over a hundred pounds of metal and glass—rested on a massive tripod, its presence both commanding and unnatural beneath the arena's balmy haze. Four large battery boxes, each a leaden anchor, stood by its side, ready to drive the mechanism that would capture more than just light and motion.

Frank Fillis, ever the ringmaster of this imperial spectacle, had gathered the entire cast. Around the arena, Matabele, Zulu, Swazi, and Basuto performers stood in expectant silence. Texas Jack, lounging against the arena seating barrier, watched with a sharp, knowing glint in his eyes, as if anticipating a show within the show. Jacob Johnson, his broad frame imposing, stood motionless beside Pasha, his deep breaths steady and measured. In the shadows, Bandini Thorburn, a young Swazi, stared wide-eyed at the camera, his small hands clenching and unclenching as though sensing something beyond the spectacle—the uncanny power of a thing that could steal a man's face and hold it captive.

Rosenthal placed a reverent hand on the machine, the theatricality of the moment deliberate. "This Biograph," he declared, his voice swelling with purpose, "is more than a camera. It is history."

He let the words settle. Some of the older men cast uncertain glances at the machine, the flickering torchlight catching the wary set of their mouths. A few shifted their footing as if resisting the urge to step back. Stories had long whispered through their lands about devices that could steal something unseen—the breath of a soul, the essence of a man.

Rosenthal continued, undeterred. "Tomorrow, we will film Major Wilson's Last Stand. Every moment, every movement, every war cry—captured forever. And with it, gentlemen, so will you."

A ripple of unease passed through the crowd.

He turned sharply. "Texas Jack," he called, fixing his gaze on the American scout, "you shall be Frederick Russell Burnham, Chief of Scouts—sharp-eyed and untouchable."

Jack gave a slow nod, his fingers brushing the brim of his hat.

Rosenthal's eyes swept the gathered men before settling on one. "Lobengula, you will play your father—the great King Lobengula."

A subtle shift passed through the group. All eyes flickered toward the tall, enigmatic figure standing apart from the others.

Lobengula, ever inscrutable, held Rosenthal's gaze for a long moment. He neither accepted nor rejected the role; he simply nodded—a gesture that was neither obedience nor defiance. The weight of his presence filled the space between them.

The question had long hung in the air, unspoken yet ever-present—*Was he truly the son of Lobengula?* Some whispered that his claim was truth, a bloodline shattered but unbroken. Others dismissed it as nothing more than Fillis's grand illusion, another layer of theatre draped over a man who had learned to wear mystery like a second skin. If Lobengula himself cared to confirm or deny it, he never had. Silence had served him better than words ever could.

Pasha watched him closely. There was something about the way he carried himself—an ease that neither invited belief nor dispelled it. Perhaps the truth didn't matter. The audience had already made up its mind.

Rosenthal pressed on. "Fillis," he gestured toward the impresario in the background, "will play Major Allan Wilson. Cecil William Coleman shall be Captain Greenless."

Fillis, arms folded, barely acknowledged the announcement. His focus lay elsewhere, calculating, already considering how best to orchestrate the spectacle.

Rosenthal's gaze swept back over the assembled men. "And the rest of you—Zulu, Matabele, Swazi—you will be the Matabele warriors. Attackers. The indomitable force against the Empire's brave last stand."

A quiet irony settled over the space, thick as dust in the lamplight.

Pasha felt uneasy. They were to become their own ghosts—warriors in name, actors in practice, assigned the role of their ancestors, yet stripped of their stories. They would charge, fall, and rise again, not in battle but for the camera's insatiable hunger. This time, their fight was not for land or honour but for spectacle, their images soon to flicker across screens in London's drawing rooms, exoticized, consumed, and repurposed for an audience that would never understand.

And The Beast—the great Biograph—would capture it all.

REELS OF ILLUSION

The gates of Earl's Court stood locked, their iron bars casting long, fractured shadows over the worn pavement. A bold-lettered poster stretched taut across the entrance:

"Closed for One Day Only – Filming in Progress."

Inside the showground, the grandstands stood eerily empty, their usual hum of spectators replaced by the distant calls of workmen. Morning sunlight slanted through the hazy mid-August sky, casting a golden glow across the arena. Though the summer of 1899 still clung to London, its heat pressing down in waves, a different storm was building beyond these walls. The Boer War loomed on the horizon, its shadow stretching across the Empire.

At the centre of the arena, the Biograph camera stood like a mechanical beast, its brass and wood frame gleaming in the morning light. The apparatus was heavy, a hulking contraption that demanded stillness and precision. Mounted on a reinforced tripod, it was more than a machine; it was an unblinking witness, ready to consume every movement, every moment, every manufactured truth.

Joseph Rosenthal moved with sharp efficiency, adjusting the frame and checking the focus. The camera's ground glass screen reflected a grainy, reversed image of the arena, flickering with ghostlike imprecision. The viewfinder vanished once the film magazine was sealed, leaving only the operator's steady hand to capture the illusion. Every detail had to be perfect. There were no second chances.

The arena took shape.

On one side, British soldiers assembled, their uniforms a mix of khaki and navy, their rifles slung loosely over their shoulders. At their centre stood their leader, revolver holstered, his stance deliberately rigid. Around them, a makeshift barricade— wooden crates, overturned wagons, scattered props—was arranged to resemble a desperate last stand.

Opposite them, the Matabele warriors stood, their spears and shields catching the light. Among them was Pasha, his bare feet pressing into the dirt, his spear poised. His body was taut, his breath steady, his mind turning over the motions that had been drilled into him.

A film technician slid the film magazine into place with a soft click. The camera's shutter was now sealed, its lens fixed, its framing unchangeable. No adjustments. No corrections. The scene would unfold exactly as planned.

Rosenthal raised his hand. A moment of absolute stillness.

Then—the camera operator started to crank the Biograph.

A bugle sounded.

The British soldiers raised their rifles, firing blank cartridges, their sharp cracks ricocheting through the arena. Smoke curled in thin ribbons from the rifles.

And then—the charge.

From across the arena, a wave of Matabele warriors surged forward, their war cries echoing against the empty arena seats. Dust rose beneath their feet, billowing into a golden haze, softening their edges and turning them into silhouettes against the light.

The battle was an illusion, a carefully rehearsed dance. Soldiers collapsed in exaggerated falls, their rifles slipping from their hands as they hit the dirt. The Matabele pressed forward, their spears thrusting in coordinated, practised arcs.

Pasha was among them. His every move was rehearsed to the second. His spear lunged forward—stopping inches from its target—an illusion of violence, perfected over weeks of repetition.

The camera whirred steadily, capturing each frame at sixteen flickering images per second.

The British fell back, scrambling toward the barricade. Their leader—Frank Fillis, cast as Major Wilson—climbed onto a heap of sandbags, revolver raised high. His coat was streaked with dust, his face set in grim defiance as he fired his final, imaginary shots.

The Matabele warriors closed in.

Shields clashed against makeshift defences. Spears flashed in the morning sun.

Pasha moved with the pack, raising his spear as he scaled the barricade. Every motion was measured and controlled—designed for spectacle, not war.

Fillis collapsed in a dramatic heap, his body crumpling atop the barricade as the warriors overtook him. The dust hung suspended in the air, catching the light like powdered gold.

The camera operator slowed the crank of the Biograph.

The final frame flickered through the shutter.

The film ran out.

The arena held its pose for a moment—bodies frozen in their carefully staged tableau. Then, the illusion dissolved.

Rosenthal exhaled, stepping back as the technicians moved in and carefully rewound the film into its cartridge. The silver halide grains of the delicate 35mm stock now held the entire battle—a flickering, ghostly imprint of dust, bodies, and spectacle.

Around them, the performers began to stir. The Matabele warriors lowered their spears, their war cries fading into low murmurs, laughter, and handshakes. The British soldiers dusted off their coats, some joking about their own "deaths." The battle had lasted mere minutes, yet soon it would be replayed endlessly, larger than life, across theatre screens across the Empire.

Rosenthal turned toward the camera.

Through its lens, history had been reshaped. The Empire had its final stand, doomed heroes, and noble savages—captured, sealed, and ready for projection.

The crew packed away the equipment. The dust settled. The gates of Earl's Court would reopen, and the grandeur of "Savage South Africa" would resume.

But tonight, history belonged to the Biograph.

SHADOWS ON THE SCREEN

Newcastle Street buzzed with life as the performers of *Savage South Africa* gathered outside the Olympic Theatre. The gaslights cast their glow over the damp cobblestones, reflecting off polished boots and brass buttons. Above them, stretched across the theatre's grand entrance, a poster proclaimed:

"Major Wilson's Last Stand: A Cinematic Triumph! Starring the Performers of *Savage South Africa*.

See the Heroes of Empire Immortalized on Film!

For One Week Only: September 5–12, 1899."

Pasha stood at the edge of the crowd, arms crossed. His eyes lingered on one word "Immortalized." It hung in the air, weighty, full of promise—but what kind of immortality was this? A flickering shadow on a wall, a carefully constructed illusion?

The British soldiers jostled each other, laughing as they reminisced about their finest "deaths" on set. One reenacted his demise dramatically, clutching his chest and staggering backwards before collapsing against a fellow soldier, who shoved him off with a snort.

"Damn fine form, old chap!" one of them teased. *"You should've been on the stage—what a waste of a man in uniform!"*

"If this film business takes off, I might consider a career shift," another quipped.

"Only if they pay in gin," someone added to a round of chuckles.

Hendrik Malan spat onto the cobblestones, shaking his head. *"'n Boer in 'n blou baadjie,"* he muttered. *"My pa sou my doodmaak."* (A Boer in a blue jacket. My father would kill me.)
Beside him, Pieter de Wet chuckled darkly. *"Ons lyk : ons eie vyande."* (We look like our own enemies.)
Malan let out a humourless laugh. *"Nee, Pieter,"* he said, voice edged with dry contempt. *"Ons lyk soos Engelse drome."* (No, Pieter. We look like English dreams.)

They weren't bitter—just bemused at the absurdity of it all.

A ripple of giggles rose from the Zulu and Swazi performers. They, too, had played roles that were not their own, dressed as Matabele warriors for the re-enactment. One of the Swazi men mimed the stiff, exaggerated charge they had performed for the cameras, drawing muffled laughter from the others.

"Siyahlekisa ngalokhu!"
(*This makes us laugh!*)

"Ngibuka mina! Angifani neNdebele!"
(*Look at me! I don't even look like a Ndebele!*)

The theatre doors were opened by a man in a top hat, and the group was ushered inside.

The theatre was dimly lit, its ceiling and walls adorned with curling plasterwork and heavy drapes. The performers of *Savage South Africa* settled into the rows of wooden seats, their whispers fading into a hush as anticipation thickened.

In the orchestra pit, musicians adjusted their sheet music. A pianist cracked his knuckles. A violinist tilted his instrument under his chin, bow poised. The flickering light of the foot lamps glowed against their faces as the conductor raised his baton.

At the back of the room, the Biograph projector whirred into life. Its heavy gears turned, and a beam of light cut through the darkness, illuminating the dust swirling in the air. The first flickering images appeared on the screen.

The dust and chaos of Earl's Court unfolded in black and white.

The British soldiers stood rigid behind their barricade, rifles at the ready, faces set in tense determination. Their uniforms—a mix of navy and khaki—looked oddly pristine, the camera's flat gaze smoothing out the dirt and sweat of real battle. Their bodies were frozen in that moment before the storm—a theatrical calm before the inevitable charge.

The Boers shifted in their seats, watching themselves play a part they never asked for.

"Kyk hoe lyk ons. So dramaties."
(*Look at us. So dramatic.*)

"Die Engelse sal sê ons's dapper."
(*The English will say we're brave.*)

"Dis 'n fokken pantomime."
(*This is a fucking pantomime.*)

Then, the attack began.

The screen image shook as the Matabele warriors—played by a mix of Zulu, Swazi, and Matabele performers—surged forward.

Their bodies moved in jerky, flickering strides, distorted by the frame rate. Spears gleamed, shields lifted, and dust churned beneath their feet.

Pasha saw himself onscreen, darting between the fighters, his spear raised high. The British rifles jerked backwards with the illusion of recoil, tiny bursts of white appearing at their muzzles, silent flashes frozen in time.

A pianist in the orchestra pit struck the keys sharply—a staccato, jarring rhythm that mimicked the crack of unseen gunfire. The violinist followed, bowing long, rising notes that hummed with tension, a musical stand-in for the chaos.

The British soldiers fell theatrically—some dropping instantly, others staggering backwards - hit by invisible bullets. One collapsed dramatically onto another, his hat tumbling off, a death far too exaggerated even for the stage.

The Zulu and Swazi performers snickered.

"Kubonakala sengathi siwukudlala lapha."
(It looks like we are just playing here.)

One of the Swazi men pointed at himself onscreen. "Bheka mina! Ngizishaya njengendoda enkulu!"
(Look at me! I fight like a great warrior!)

The laughter rippled outward, a soft, mocking chorus that the British performers did not share.

The orchestra swelled—violins trembling, the piano climbing into a hurried, erratic tempo.

The battle reached its climax. The British, backs against their barricade, fired their final shots. A bugle call rang through the orchestra pit, a desperate wail, as Major Wilson—played by Frank Fillis—clambered atop the barricade, revolver raised.

His uniform was streaked with dust, his movements grandiose. He fired once, twice, then stumbled back. The camera captured his perfect fall—arms outstretched, head tilted just so, as if descending into martyrdom.

The Matabele warriors swarmed. The last British soldier fell.

The final frame froze—a still image of the battle's aftermath, black-and-white figures suspended in the projector's glow.

Then—darkness.

The film reel spun empty, and the projector stuttered into silence.

For a moment, no one moved.

Then, the theatre stirred.

The British performers clapped, nodding in approval. One officer near the front turned to his companions.

"Jolly good show."

The Boers were less impressed. One mimicked Fillis' exaggerated death, lurching backwards in his seat with a groan. His companion barked a laugh.

"So veel vir ons geskiedenis."
(*So much for our history.*)

The Zulu and Swazi performers were still murmuring among themselves, half-laughing, half-bemused.

Pasha stayed seated, fists clenched on his knees. The screen had gone dark, but the ghost of himself lingered—forever frozen in a white man's version of Africa. He had not just played a warrior; he had become a phantom. A curiosity. A shadow flickering between history and myth.

Outside, Newcastle Street was alight with gas lamps, their warm glow spilling onto the cobblestones as the performers vanished into the night.

The British laughed. The Boers scoffed.

Pasha turned away.

A shadow flickering between history and myth.

SCANDALS OF "THE KRAAL"

The Big Zulu's roar shattered the uneasy calm of Lillie Road, its raw power reverberating through the cold October night. It was the kind of sound that made even those accustomed to the unpredictable energy of the city pause, a deep, guttural bellow that carried both warning and fury.

Police Constable Pullen, rounding the corner, found himself stumbling into a scene of utter chaos—a brawl spilling across the street, fists swinging wildly, the sharp crack of bone against flesh punctuating the air as men grappled and cursed in a tangle of limbs. The performers of *Savage South Africa* were at its centre, their bodies moving with a raw, unrestrained aggression that had nothing to do with the choreographed battles they performed daily.

Towering above them was Jacob Johnson, the Big Zulu, his broad chest bare in the freezing air, his breath fogging as he struggled to separate the warring factions, his booming commands in Zulu drowned by the scuffle. His presence alone was enough to still lesser men, but tonight, the flames of anger burned too high, and whatever had ignited the fight had already consumed reason.

Pullen's shout cut across the scene, his voice edged with authority. *"Enough of this! Stand down at once!"*

The combatants barely acknowledged him, their rage too consuming, their focus narrowed to the grudges they sought to settle with their fists.

Then Johnson turned, his dark, piercing gaze locking onto the constable. The air seemed to tighten, a silent weight pressing down before the words came—low, deliberate, thick with disdain.

"Dirty white man."

The insult struck like a lash. Pullen's jaw clenched, his face darkening. With a snarl, he yanked his truncheon free, the polished wood flashing in the lamplight as he lunged forward.

Johnson was ready. As Pullen swung, the Big Zulu's arm shot up, absorbing the blow with the ease of a man who had weathered far worse. The crack of wood against hardened muscle rang out, but Johnson barely flinched. In the same fluid motion, he seized Pullen's wrist, twisted hard, and drove him backwards.

The constable hit the ground with a grunt, the impact forcing the breath from his lungs. His truncheon skidded across the cobblestones, useless now, as Johnson loomed over him, unmoving but undeniable.

The moment that followed was grotesque in its ferocity. Johnson pinned Pullen beneath him. His teeth flashed—then sank deep into the constable's nose. The scream that tore from Pullen's throat was a sound neither words nor imagination could fully capture, his hands scrabbling in vain to push the Zulu away as blood poured from his nose onto the icy street.

Two constables arrived as Pullen staggered upright. Blood streamed from his nose. He barely managed to choke out the order.

"Get him!"

The officers lunged, grappling with Johnson, their arms locking around his shoulders in a desperate attempt to restrain him. But the Big Zulu was all muscle and momentum. With a roar, he twisted free, sending one constable sprawling onto the cobblestones. The other clung on, struggling to drag him down. Johnson heaved forward, dragging the officer with him like dead weight, his strength unchecked.

Then the chase began.

Boots thundered against the slick stones, pursuit ringing down the narrow streets as two more constables arrived, their shouts cutting through the night. Johnson tore through the alleyways, his breath ragged, his massive frame barrelling toward escape. But the streets twisted against him—blind corners, dead ends. The city closed in.

The constables closed the gap.

They cornered him near a row of shuttered shopfronts. Johnson spun, fists raised, ready for the fight he knew was coming. The first officer lunged—he sent him crashing back with a single blow. The second struck with his truncheon—Johnson caught his wrist mid-swing, wrenched it sideways, and the man yelped in pain.

But three against one was too much, even for him.

Pullen, face slick with blood, hurled himself into the fray, and the weight of numbers finally dragged Johnson down. He thrashed and fought, but hands gripped his arms and his legs, forcing him against the cold, unforgiving stone.

The clatter of handcuffs snapped against the night.

The newspapers wasted no time. By morning, London's press had already seized upon the savagery of the attack, their headlines blaring sensational accounts of a *"Zulu's Bloodlust at Earl's Court"* and *"Constable Mauled in Barbaric Assault."*

Jacob Johnson stood in the dock; the West London Police Court was packed to the rafters, a dense crowd pressing into every available space, craning to glimpse the man who had sent an English policeman to the surgeon's table.

He stood tall, unbowed, unrepentant, his broad shoulders squared as he faced his accusers. Though he spoke English well enough, he refused to use it, answering only in Zulu, his voice carrying a deliberate, measured weight that made each syllable seem more defiant than the last.

The interpreter, standing beside him, swallowed visibly before translating. *"He does not deny the fight. He says he was struck first."*

From the witness stand, Constable Pullen, his nose heavily bandaged, flushed a deep shade of red, his hands gripping the wooden railing with white-knuckled fury.

"Lies!" he spat, his voice trembling with indignation. *"Lies, Your Worship! He bit me like a—like a rabid animal!"*

The magistrate, seated high above the courtroom, barely raised an eyebrow at the outburst. Instead, he turned his gaze back to Johnson, his expression unreadable.

"He is not an Englishman, he does not understand our laws or our customs. These are matters that must be considered."

A pause.

Then, the verdict.

"A fine of three pounds, or fourteen days in prison."

The gavel struck wood.

A murmur rippled through the room, hushed but heavy with opinion. In the gallery, a cluster of Boers, arms crossed, and faces set like stone, exchanged looks of contempt.

"'n Skande," one of them muttered under his breath. *A disgrace.*

Johnson did not flinch. As he was led from the dock, his back remained straight, his face an unreadable mask.

For most in the courtroom, the ruling was a mere legal affair, another criminal subdued.

But for Pasha, sitting silently among the crowd, it was something far more profound—a crack in the illusion, a moment when the men of Savage South Africa were no longer just performers, no longer just entertainment, but something more—something real, something dangerous.

The following weeks saw *Savage South Africa* descend deeper into scandal, the carefully curated spectacle unravelling with every new headline, each fresh outrage another thread pulled from the fabric of the illusion. What had once been billed as a grand imperial display was now the subject of salacious gossip, whispered in drawing rooms, scorned in editorials, and dissected in pubs where men read the newspapers aloud with exaggerated relish.

The city, already uneasy with the distant rumblings of war, had turned its attention to the chaos brewing behind the fences of *Savage South Africa*.

More signs of the show unravelling came with Edith Burston and Ella Gray, two young women of respectable background, who had been discovered drunk and disorderly on Lillie Road, their laughter spilling into the night as they clung to Jacob Johnson's powerful frame. He had become a figure of both fascination and scandal since his trial, his name spoken in equal parts admiration and condemnation, a man who, in the eyes of London's more respectable citizens, had already been marked as a savage beyond taming.

That night, fuelled by drink and emboldened by the reckless euphoria of their own defiance, the women clung to Johnson's arms, laughing, swaying, their skirts brushing against his legs as they paraded through the gaslit streets. Their voices rang out in playful shrieks, their heads thrown back in raucous amusement, the world around them be damned.

But not everyone found it entertaining.

A group of men emerged from the shadows, their faces set, their stance rigid with unspoken hostility. One of them stepped forward, his voice low, edged with warning.

"Leave the white women alone."

Johnson grinned. The tension in the air was thick, but he felt no fear—only the heat of whisky in his veins and the roaring delight of the spectacle. He let the moment hang, then slowly lifted his fighting stick, twirling it in exaggerated flourishes, his movements playful and theatrical.

The women shrieked with laughter, clutching his arms tighter, their amusement ringing through the street.

Johnson bared his teeth in a wide, exaggerated grin, rolling his shoulders, puffing out his chest like a warrior before battle. "What, afraid of a little show?" he boomed, his deep laughter rolling over them like distant thunder.

The men hesitated. For all their posturing, something about how he carried himself—too bold, too sure, too much a spectacle—unnerved them. He was no meek outsider. He was performing the very thing they feared, mocking their anger with every twirl of his stick, every bark of laughter.

One of the men spat onto the cobbles, and another clenched his fists but did not move forward. The moment teetered on the edge of something darker.

Johnson gave one final flourish, letting the stick rest against his shoulder.

The moment the constables arrived, the night collapsed into something else—no longer laughter, no longer defiance, but something colder, something irreversible. The women's shrieks of amusement turned to protests, their hands still gripping

Johnson's arms as if to tether the moment before it shattered completely.

But the law was swift.

Dragged from the gaslit streets into the harsh glare of the magistrate's court, the spectacle did not end—it only changed stages. Johnson stood before the judge with the same unshaken presence, his broad shoulders squared, his expression unreadable. The magistrate's warning rang out—stern, deliberate, but without a fine. A performance, perhaps, for those gathered to watch.

The women were not so lucky. Their names—already whispered with scandal—were now etched in ink, splashed across the morning papers. The judgement fell on them like an iron gate slamming shut. Four shillings each. Not a ruinous sum, but enough to mark them. Enough to stain their reputations in ways that no fine could erase.

By the time they left the courthouse, their laughter had long since faded. What had begun as a night of reckless amusement had ended as a warning—one that neither of them would soon forget.

Then came the incident that truly shattered the illusion, which sent London into an uproar.

Seventeen-year-old Anne Maude Higgs, a girl of decent upbringing, had disappeared into the *Savage South Africa* grounds, slipping beyond the fences, lingering where no proper young woman should. Her mother, distraught and inconsolable, stood before the magistrate, barely able to speak, her voice raw with grief and humiliation as she declared that her daughter had been keeping company with an African performer.

That was all that needed to be said.

The newspapers seized upon the story like wolves descending upon fresh blood. *A White Girl's Ruin in the Hands of Savages*, they screamed, their inked words dripping with the kind of manufactured horror that sold papers by the thousands.

The Daily Chronicle and *The Pall Mall Gazette* filled their front pages with ominous warnings of the moral degradation festering behind the fences of *Savage South Africa*, declaring it a breeding ground for corruption, temptation, and ruin.

Missionaries took up the cry, standing in pulpits, thundering against the wickedness that had infiltrated Earl's Court. The warnings grew ever more fevered, and their sermons were thick with the stench of righteous indignation.

Despite the scandal that erupted in the press and the outrage her disappearance ignited, Anne Maude Higgs later testified that she had gone to the Savage South Africa grounds of her own free will. She had not been abducted, coerced, or held against her will, as the newspapers had so eagerly suggested. The feverish headlines that painted her as a victim of predatory savagery unravelled under scrutiny.

Eventually, Anne returned home without incident, her life resuming much as before—though her name, for a time, remained a cautionary whisper in the parlours of respectable society. Yet, the damage had already been done. The press had fed its frenzy, the moral panic had run its course, and London had its scandal. The truth, quieter and far less salacious, was of little interest to those who had already decided.

Inside the Kraal, Pasha watched it all unfold. He saw the performers' faces shift from quiet amusement to unease, from bemusement to something darker that felt too much like being hunted. He saw the whispers tighten into something sharper, something that no longer danced at the edges but pressed inward, coiling around them.

The fences had always been there, framing their world, defining their existence within the boundaries set for them by men who decided what London would see, what it would believe, what it would accept.

But now, those fences no longer felt like a performance space.

They felt like walls.

And beyond them, the city, restless, watching, eager for the next scandal, the next humiliation, the next piece of evidence to confirm the growing unease that *Savage South Africa* was no longer just an exhibition but something far more dangerous—a challenge, a question, an unwanted truth that could not be controlled much longer.

BITTER WATERS

October 1899.

The Northampton sky hung low, its heavy clouds casting a gloom over the cobbled streets. Inside the courthouse, Pasha sat in the dock, his hands clasped tightly in his lap, his gaze fixed on a crack in the stone floor. The magistrate's words rose and fell around him, a rhythmic tide of judgment and sympathy. His crime—attempting to take his own life—was read aloud for the record. To the court, it was not despair but an act of defiance against life, which demanded correction. The verdict carried mercy: instead of prison, Pasha was placed in the care of the prison chaplain, a man whose reputation for patience preceded him.

The journey that had brought him here felt as fragmented as the crack he now studied. Just weeks earlier, Pasha had been part of the Savage South Africa show, performing alongside warriors, dancers, and animals in a spectacle that blurred reality and reenactment. But the show had begun to crumble from within.

In early October, the camp at Earl's Court was rife with scandal after a Zulu performer, in a drunken rage, bit a police officer's nose during a skirmish. The incident made headlines, casting a shadow over an enterprise already fraying at the edges. Word soon spread that the show would close by the end of the month. Performers whispered of unpaid wages and imminent departures.

For Pasha, the unravelling of the show mirrored his own. The life he had known in the Kraal—a life of performance and pretence—no longer held him. On October 12, he slipped away, leaving the dust and noise of Earl's Court behind. Northampton became his destination, drawn there by the memory of a girl he had met months earlier. Her name was Mary, and in her company, Pasha had found a fleeting sense of ease, a reprieve from the relentless churn of the show. He hoped that Northampton might offer more than solace; it might offer belonging.

But Northampton was not the haven he had imagined. Mary had liked his stories at first—the way he spoke of the Kraal, of battles and warriors, of a life larger than this grey town. But the stories turned heavier. He turned heavier. And when the bottle did the talking, she stopped listening.

Then, on the night of October 19, it ended.

Their argument had been brief, sharp-edged. Mary's patience had worn thin, and Pasha, weary and restless, didn't fight to stay. He shoved his few belongings into a small bag, slinging it over his shoulder. There was nothing left to say.

In the kitchen, he reached for the bottle of gin—the only thing that had never turned its back on him. As he lifted it, his eyes landed on the drain cleaner sitting beside the basin. A cleaner. A chemical meant to strip away stains – unblock drains. Without thinking, he grabbed it.

Mary stood in the doorway, arms folded tight. She didn't try to stop him. As he stepped outside, the door slammed shut behind him, the sound final, echoing in the empty street.

He walked. The night was cold, and the town was silent. He took a swig of gin, the warmth barely touching him. Then, on some deserted corner, he twisted open the second bottle.

The acrid scent hit first, burning his nostrils, sharper than regret. Then came the swallow—a raw, searing agony clawing down his throat, into his gut, twisting his insides into something unrecognisable. The world tilted. His legs buckled. The pavement rushed up to meet him.

By morning, a passerby found him slumped in the gutter, the bottle still clutched in his hand.

The constables were called, and while the doctor managed to save his life, the law demanded its due. He was arrested, charged with attempted suicide, and brought to the courthouse on October 20. The trial was brief, and the courtroom was cold and austere.

"Pasha of Mafeteng, this court finds you guilty of self-destruction. The law cannot abide such defiance." The magistrate's voice was steady, neither cruel nor kind. "However, in light of your circumstances, we grant you mercy, Mercy." The word felt like an unfamiliar taste on Pasha's tongue.

And so, he was released into the care of Mr. Batchelor, the prison chaplain.

The chaplain's quarters smelled of old wood and candle wax. A modest fire crackled in the hearth—not roaring, not weak, just steady. A fire that endured. The chaplain did not preach, did not scold, did not ask questions. He simply existed. And in the silence, something in Pasha began to settle. For Pasha, the days blurred together, each one an uneasy truce with his thoughts. Northampton, which had promised him renewal, had delivered him to this strange limbo instead.

But the chaplain's calm began to penetrate Pasha's spirit. He watched the firelight flicker against the walls, its dance both fragile and enduring. His mind returned to Mafeteng, to the clean air of the highlands and the life he had left behind. On a cold November evening, as the wind howled outside, news reached Pasha of the SS Adalia. The ship, bound for Cape Town, was set to leave Southampton on November 8. It was to carry performers and workers from the show, a final exodus from England to Africa. The thought of it stirred something in Pasha—a pull toward the continent that had shaped him, toward the hills he still saw in his dreams.

On the evening of November 7, with a pouch of coins from the chaplain jingling faintly in his pocket, Pasha boarded the train from Northampton. The platform was wrapped in mist, a thick grey that clung to the edges of the world. He thought of Mafeteng—of air so sharp it cut clean, of the blue that stretched unbroken above the hills. This fog was not his. This place was not his. But the train was moving. And that, at least, meant something.

Pasha sat by the window, the countryside slipping past in hues of ochre and grey. He thought of Mary, Earl's Court, and the strange, winding road that had brought him here. But as the train carried him southward, the weight of those memories began to lift, replaced by the faint stirrings of hope.

THE VOYAGE HOME

The grand lights of Earl's Court flickered out, leaving behind only silence and the whispers of scandal clinging to the empty stage. Where once the Kraal had roared with spectacle, now only the wind moved through its abandoned structures. For some, the show would go on—new contracts would be inked, and new stages would be set at Olympia.

To the show's management, performers were numbers, not people. Ink on a ledger decided who stayed and who was discarded. The Zulus and Swazis, with their towering forms and ceremonial spears, remained. The rest were erased, their contracts severed without a second thought. The pageantry that had once elevated them in the imperial imagination now reduced them to little more than forgotten players, their stories left to sink into the shadows of history.

It had been 25 days since the first salvo of the Boer War was fired on October 12, 1899, marking the beginning of a conflict that would reshape South Africa. Now, on November 8, the docks at Southampton bristled with the energy of departure. The "Adalia" had been hired to ferry the performers home, its modest frame dwarfed by the weight of its passengers and their untold stories.

Among the 72 performers preparing to depart England, the divide was glaring. The 23 Boers—settlers and skirmishers who had played their parts with grim determination—were ushered into cabins above deck. Their names were carefully inked into the ship's manifest, reflecting their perceived importance. In stark contrast, the 49 African performers—four Cape Girls, two Hottentot women, 25 Coleman's Boys, and eight Cape Boys—were consigned to steerage. Listed collectively as "circus followers," their identities were scrawled informally, if at all, as though they were just another line item in the cargo manifest.

Pasha watched the scene unfold, standing silently on the gangplank. Each step he took echoed with the weight of what had passed and what lay ahead. London's applause and the bright lights of the stage now felt like distant memories, replaced by the low murmur of unease among the passengers. Above deck, the Boers moved into their assigned quarters; their journey charted with meticulous care. Below the deck, the conditions tell a different story.

The air below deck was thick—sweat, damp wood, and the slow rot of seawater. Pasha sat apart, his stomach tightening with every lurch of the ship, the floor beneath him groaning. The Cape Boys jostled for space, their sharp words cutting through the restless din. The Coleman Boys sprawled across the wooden floors, their voices weaving shared stories into a fragile thread of unity. The Cape Girls and Hottentot women huddled together, their muted laughter a quiet rebellion against the oppressive atmosphere.

As the *Adalia* pulled away from the docks, its horn bellowed a final farewell to England's cold, grey shores. Pasha stood at the railing, the wind clawing at his coat as he watched the coastline dissolve into mist. The last time he had made this journey, there had been a flicker of adventure, the illusion of something grand.

Now, there was only the weight of failure and the unknown road ahead.

The voyage stretched longer than expected. The ship lingered in foreign ports, caught in the slow rhythms of trade and tide. Below deck, time blurred—the same cramped space, the same restless waiting. As the *Adalia* pressed southward, the air thickened with heat, the sea darkening toward Africa.

By the time they reached the southern seas, something in the air had shifted. The Cape Boys grew quiet, their movements tense, bracing for whatever awaited them. The Hottentot women and Cape Girls huddled together, their rare laughter edged with something unspoken.

As the first outline of Africa's coast broke the horizon, Pasha felt it settle in his bones—this was no return. No applause. No firelit welcome. No stage.

Only war.

CARRYING SHADOWS TO AFRICA

The morgue was a world of half-light and silence, the shadows thick and unmoving. The faint intermittent thuds of distant explosions and the sharp crack of sniper fire drifted through the walls, muffled but constant. Dust danced from the ceiling, a reminder of the violence that had settled over the town like a heavy shroud. Each new tremor from a nearby blast stirred the stale air, heightening the tension in the suffocating room.

The body lay sprawled on the cold, sterile table, a stark reminder of the violence that had transpired. A two-inch wound gaped in the skull, its edges jagged where the bone had given way.

The bullet had done its work mercilessly—tissue obliterated, fragments of bone driven inward. Blood, long congealed, clung in dark rivulets, a final signature of the moment life was torn away.

Dr. W. Hayes, the Principal Medical Officer, stood over the body, his expression a mixture of clinical detachment and grim resolve. His hands moved methodically, guided by the heavy weight of duty, as he prepared to dissect the tragedy before him. The air held a faint, unsettling mixture that hinted at the violence and urgency of life—a sombre backdrop to the solemn task ahead.

_____ The Day Before _____

The man's revolver glinted in the muted light of the Dixon Hotel's lobby as his arm trembled, aimed at the journalist. Time froze in that breathless moment. A sharp crack tore through the air, and the acrid smell of burnt powder filled his nostrils. In an instant, silence fell—thick, stunned, and oppressive. Ernest Parlow's eyes widened in shock before his body crumpled, blood spreading faster than comprehension.

Murdleson staggered back, the weapon still loosely in his grip. His breath came in ragged gasps as he stammered, "It was an accident. I swear it—God, I swear it was..." The assembled crowd in the lobby, who had witnessed heated words moments before, now stood frozen in disbelief at the murder that had unfolded so suddenly.

By evening, Murdleson's name whispered through the trenches, carried in low voices by officers at their fires and soldiers huddled in the barracks. The same man who had stood tall at Cannon Kopje hailed a hero just days ago, now found himself at the centre of the scandal. Mafeking, suffocating under siege, reeled from another blow. Food was scarce, tempers short, and every new death seemed heavier than the last.

The tragedy struck just days after the Boer siege began on October 13, another blow to a town already teetering on the edge.

At first light, the preliminary hearing convened, with Captain W.G. Bell presiding over a room heavy with exhaustion and suspicion. Soldiers and witnesses shuffled forward to recount the moments before the gunshot—the argument, the insults, the slow simmer of tension that had finally boiled over.

Murdleson, pale and visibly shaken, muttered his remorse. It had all happened so fast. Whispers spread through the town. Some claimed Parlow had goaded Murdleson, mocking his heroism at Cannon Kopje. Others said the siege had broken him, the pressure snapping something inside.

The investigation was only beginning, but the tragedy had already become the town's pulse—a dark current beneath the surface, adding to the suffocating pressure of the Boer siege.

But far across the sea, Pasha sailed blind to it all—the gunshot, the trial, the town gasping under siege. Mafeking's dead meant nothing to the waves carrying him forward. The applause was behind him. Ahead, war waited.

A NAME REDUCED TO INK

Stepping off the "Adalia" at Cape Town, Pasha felt the energy of the quay—traders, soldiers, and workers shouting, bargaining, ordering. A young boy perched on a wooden crate caught his attention. He held up a fresh copy of The Cape Argus.

"Siege of Mafeking Continues! Scouts Wanted!" the boy called, his voice cutting through the dockside din with startling clarity.

Digging a coin from his pocket, Pasha approached, and the boy handed him the paper with a wide-eyed grin. He unfolded the paper - the bold headlines slashing across the page like knife strokes: "Mafeking Siege Continues: Boer Forces Close In. British Flying Column Advancing."

His breath caught in his throat. This was it—the war had reached the heart of the land he knew, and the Boers were spreading like wildfire across the veld. But what struck him most was an advertisement beneath the main article: "Native Scouts Wanted: For Service in Mafeking and Ladysmith. Apply at Local Recruitment Centres."

The seed had already been planted in Pasha's mind. He hadn't sailed across oceans to sit idly by. The war that loomed across the plains of his homeland was drawing him in like the pull of a riptide. He was ready.

"Where's the recruitment office for scouts?" he asked the boy, gesturing toward the article.

The boy pointed down the quay with a smirk. "Check at the magistrate's office near the barracks."

At the local magistrate's office on Adderley Street, Pasha was directed to a recruitment post on Wale Street, just two streets away.

As Pasha approached the small recruitment station, the sun cast deep shadows across Cape Town's streets. It had been a long, unforgiving journey back to his homeland. As he approached the station, a small group of men—some local, others from distant villages—gathered. Their faces showed signs of exhaustion, and their clothes were tattered, yet their eyes reflected a shared sense of determination.

Many of the black farm workers had watched the farms they toiled on go up in flames, their livelihoods reduced to ash by the war sweeping the land. Others had been cast out from the mines where they once laboured, left with no means to survive. When the British came recruiting, there was little choice. Pride had no place in survival.

The recruitment station was a rough, hastily assembled structure—a wooden building with a canvas roof for shade, a Union Jack fluttering lazily in the breeze. Under the shade, a storekeeper sworn in by the British army as a recruitment clerk sat behind a makeshift desk, a thick ledger open. The storekeeper, a man with thinning hair, printed the names neatly in the ledger. His shirt cuffs were stained with dust and ink.

Pasha stepped forward when his turn came.

"Name?" the storekeeper grunted, still not looking up.

"Pasha Liffey," he replied, his voice steady but carrying the weight of all he'd been through.

The storekeeper barely glanced at him before scrawling something in the ledger. Pasha leaned in just enough to see what had been scrawled: 'Liffy.' A name that was almost his but not quite, reshaped with indifference. He thought about correcting the clerk. But the man barely looked at him, his ink-stained fingers already flipping to the next blank line. At that moment, Pasha understood—he was not a person here. He was an entry in a book, a number on a list, a body to be used. "Age?" the storekeeper asked, still uninterested.

"Eighteen," Pasha answered.

"And you know what's expected of you?"

Pasha nodded. He knew. The British weren't arming their black recruits, not officially. They were scouts, runners, guides— pawns in a game far more significant than themselves. He would be expected to navigate the treacherous terrain, to lead British soldiers through the labyrinth of war, to spy on Boer movements, and to receive and deliver messages. Dangerous work but work that offered a glimmer of hope in the form of more than a soldier's wage—up to £2 a month, food included.

The storekeeper glanced up, sizing Pasha up with a single sweep of his tired eyes. "You'll report tomorrow at first light. You'll board a train heading north and meet a British contingent heading for Mafeking."

"And hey, Liffy—consider yourself lucky. You could ask for more as a messenger... you'll see."

Pasha turned and walked out of the shack, the weight of the storekeeper's indifference pressing down on him like a heavy cloak.

As Pasha walked back toward the city centre, his thoughts turned to his father, the missionaries who had taught him to read, and the Fraser brothers who had taken him to England. And then he thought of the "Savage South Africa" show, of the way he had fought in the reenactments, playing the part of the warrior, the savage, for the entertainment of British crowds. The irony of it all wasn't lost on him. Here he was, a man who had once performed the role of a warrior in a theatre, now preparing to become one for real.

The next day, Pasha boarded the train heading toward Mafeking. The train lurched forward, the rhythmic clatter of the wheels hammering out a steady march toward war. He had left England behind. Now, with every mile, he left something else—whatever part of himself had once believed he could stay untouched by this war. As the sun set, the train halted at a temporary military siding. He disembarked with a group of recruits. A corporal stood waiting, his moustache waxed into precise points, his uniform crisp despite the heat. He scanned the recruits like a man appraising livestock. Clearing his throat, he spat onto the ground, then spoke as if reading from a script. "You'll be posted at a heliograph and carrier pigeon station." His tone was flat, practised—he had done this many times before, and he would do it again long after these men were dead or forgotten. "There will be overnight or week-long stays in Mafeking. Tomorrow, I'll show you the ropes."

The corporal paused, "We'll march 110 miles from here before we reach the 50-mile zone outside Mafeking, where you'll be deployed. We move with the relief column. You'll be posted at your station once we're within the 50-mile zone."

Pasha absorbed the words. The reality of it all was starting to hit. No more applause, no more performances. This was the beginning of something darker, something real.

As night fell, Pasha felt a stirring deep within him—a flicker of hope, a spark of resilience that had never left him, even in the darkest moments of his life. He had survived so much already. And now, as he prepared to fight again, this time for the British, he knew one thing for sure: no matter how the war twisted and turned, no matter how the world sought to reshape him, Pasha Liffey would remain standing.

Because surviving was what he did. And tomorrow, the war would begin—not in stories, not on stages. But in blood, in dust, in the merciless stretch of the veld.

THE BELL-RINGING HERO

Pasha crouched on the stoep floor of the Mafeking post office, the sun warming his back as he adjusted the pouch slung across his shoulder. It was his first assignment as a runner, paired with a Barolong scout for a mission that would take them beyond the town's brittle safety. Around him, a group of messengers gathered in a loose circle, swapping stories with the easy camaraderie of men who had seen too much and yet managed to laugh through it.

"You've heard about General Snyman, haven't you?" one of them said, his grin infectious. Pasha glanced up, catching the glint of mischief in the runner's eyes. "Not the Boer, the baboon!" A ripple of laughter spread through the group. Before Pasha could ask, a younger boy sprang up to mimic the infamous creature's antics. He skittered across the stoep, long arms flailing like a clumsy marionette before letting out an exaggerated yelp and scrambling for an invisible bell. The others erupted into applause, doubling over as the reenactment climaxed.

Pasha couldn't help but chuckle. The absurdity of relying on a bell-ringing baboon to save lives during a siege seemed fitting for a place like Mafeking, where normalcy had long since surrendered to survival. "Imagine that", one runner snorted, wiping a tear from his eye. "A baboon with more sense than General Snyman and faster legs than any of us!"

"And the best part?" another chimed in, his voice rising above the laughter. "The baboon never misses—rings the bell, bolts for cover, and lives to do it all again!"

111

The laughter was short-lived. A resounding, metallic thud from the hills cut through the air—the unmistakable echo of a Boer artillery shell being fired. Conversations stopped mid-sentence, heads snapping toward the watchtower. There, perched on his platform like a sentry, was General Snyman—Mafeking's furry saviour.

With uncanny agility, the baboon climbed to his post, his sharp eyes scanning the horizon. And then came the familiar clang of the bell, its piercing sound a signal that had saved countless lives. As the last echoes faded, the baboon darted off, a blur of fur vanishing into the chaos before the runners scattered like startled birds.

In an instant, the stoep emptied, the men darting toward their assigned shelters. Pasha and his Barolong companion exchanged glances before joining the surge, their movements swift and instinctive. The streets came alive with the shuffle of townsfolk ducking behind walls, diving into trenches, their actions honed by months of bombardment.

The shell landed with a resounding boom just outside the town's edge. Dust and debris billowed into the air, a harmless warning shot this time, but no one paused to celebrate. Pasha crouched behind a stone wall, his breath coming fast as the dust cloud began to settle. Relief coursed through him, mixed with the unshakable tension of knowing this was just one of many to come.

The Barolong scout nudged Pasha, nodding toward the gully where their journey would begin. With a final glance at the post office, now eerily silent, Pasha adjusted the pouch across his chest. This wasn't just another day in Mafeking; it was his initiation into a role where humour, danger, and resilience blurred into a single, unrelenting reality.

And as he followed his partner into the shadows of the veld, he couldn't help but think: Only in Mafeking could a bell-ringing baboon be a hero.

MESSAGES OF HOPE AND SURVIVAL

The siege wrapped around Mafeking like an iron fist, tightening with each passing day. Beyond the crumbling walls and barbed wire, the dry veld stretched endless and unyielding, dotted with thorn bushes, sun-scorched rocks, and the distant silhouettes of Boer commando posts. The sky hung vast and indifferent, while the British defences held firm—more from necessity than strength.

Inside the town, survival was a fragile balancing act. The streets were lined with makeshift barricades, sandbags piled high against crumbling buildings. Hunger gnawed at the people, their rations growing thinner by the week. By day, they braved the scorching heat, and by night, the cold cut through every layer of cloth and skin, as if the land itself sought to wear them down.

Yet, for all the British military reports praising Mafeking's resilience, it was more than a soldier's struggle—it was a town held together by those whose stories would never reach London's front pages.

South of the defensive lines lay the Barolong Stadt, a settlement whose people had as much to lose as anyone behind British walls. Chief Wessels Montsioa and his warriors patrolled its borders, their rifles raised against the same Boer enemy that had threatened their land long before this war began. But their fight was different. They weren't fighting for the Crown or Queen; they were fighting for their homes, their families—the right to exist beyond the iron fences of an empire that barely acknowledged them.

From the Stadt, scouts ventured out under the cover of night, slipping past enemy lines with nothing but whispers and the rhythm of their own heartbeat to guide them. They carried no rifles, no spears—only messages. Intelligence scrawled on scraps of paper, tied beneath tunics, pressed against pounding chests. Theirs was a battle of shadows and silence, where every successful mission meant another day Mafeking might hold out.

In the heart of the town, in a room cluttered with loose pages and urgency, Sol Plaatje worked tirelessly. The scouts brought him hurried sketches, whispers of Boer troop movements, notes scratched onto torn scraps of paper. He translated them into something useful—something the British command could act upon.

By day, Plaatje sat at his desk in the Mafeking Mail, crafting reports for distant editors who would never feel the hunger of the siege. By night, he turned the scouts' whispered intelligence into something more vital—a lifeline of words. His hands rarely stilled, and his pen never rested. The siege moved through him, his ink shaping the chaos into order.

Yet he saw what the British dispatches omitted.

His diary—written in candlelight while shells shattered rooftops—was not just an account of war. It was an indictment. He wrote of the disparity in rations, where white civilians received better provisions than their African counterparts. He noted the unequal recognition, where Barolong scouts risked their lives but went unmentioned in military reports. He recorded the fears of his people—the growing tension, the knowledge that when relief came, it would not come for them.

And still, the town endured.

The days bled into each other, the streets thick with dust, the air heavy with smoke from the Boer bombardments that came without warning. The defenders took their positions—British soldiers at the barricades, Barolong warriors guarding their Stadt, runners disappearing into the night with messages that could save or doom them all.

Mafeking was not just a military stronghold—it was a patchwork of survival.

In the west, the Mafeking Cadet Corps, mere boys in oversized uniforms, darted through the town carrying messages and ammunition, their youthful faces set with the solemnity of men twice their age. In the east, women in makeshift hospitals stitched wounds, their hands raw from endless work. In the south, the Barolong scouts returned before dawn, their eyes hollow, their bodies aching from the miles they had run, knowing they would do it all again the next night.

Through it all, Sol Plaatje remained at his desk, listening, writing, documenting. He was not a soldier, not a scout, yet he fought in his own way—turning the siege into words, ensuring the town's struggles would not be erased by history's selective memory.

Beyond Mafeking, the veld carried the sharp scent of scorched earth, the dry air vibrating with the distant crack of gunfire. The siege pressed harder, the town's defences groaning under the strain.

But in the darkness, the runners still moved—whispering through the enemy lines, clutching words that meant life or death.

And in his room, by the dim glow of a flickering candle, Plaatje dipped his pen once more into the ink, knowing that no matter how the siege ended, history would need to remember.

FROM THE STOEP TO THE TRENCHES

March 01, 1900

The siege had a way of stretching time. Some days passed in tense silence, the town locked in a waiting game, while others erupted in chaos—booms of artillery, the sharp crack of rifle fire, the rush of orders. But then there were days when nothing happened at all, and the waiting became the battle.

Pasha sat among the runners, watching the dust swirl in the midday heat. They gathered outside the post office, sprawled on the stoep or leaning against crates, their chatter subdued as they waited for their next orders. The familiar weight of the message pouch sat against his chest, a reminder that, at any moment, a new mission could send them sprinting across the veld.

Tau, a Barolong scout who had been with the British forces since the siege began, sat in the centre of the group. His wiry frame was relaxed, but his sharp eyes missed nothing. He had the kind of presence that made men stop what they were doing and listen. Today, he was recounting the previous night's events—an operation none of the runners had witnessed, but all were eager to hear about.

"So, there we were," Tau began his voice calm but carrying the weight of the story, "just beyond the northern trenches, moving toward the Brickfields. The Boers had set up an advanced post near the kiln. It wasn't much—just a sniper position—but they'd

118

made it dangerous enough. You couldn't get within fifty yards of it without feeling their eyes on you."

The runners leaned in closer, the usual restlessness stilled by the gravity of the tale. Even Pasha, still learning the rhythm of this group, found himself drawn into the scene Tau painted, imagining the dark silhouettes of the Brickfields looming against the horizon.

"Taylor had a plan," Tau continued. "He said we'd circle through the gullies and dry riverbeds to stay out of sight. We kept low, using the natural dips and channels in the ground for cover. It wasn't much, but it was better than nothing. When we reached the edge of the kiln, it felt like we were standing in the shadow of a monster."

"The snipers?" one of the younger runners asked, his voice hushed.

"Close. Too close. You could hear them, their voices barely above whispers. They were joking softly, trying not to give away their position. One muttered something about giving the next Barolong scout a proper haircut." He paused, a grin breaking through his serious expression. "And then, just as we're crouched there, holding our breath, one of them lets out the loudest fart you've ever heard."

The group erupted into laughter, the tension breaking in an instant.

"What did you do?" someone asked between chuckles.

"What could we do?" Tau replied, shrugging. "We thought we were pinned down, trying not to laugh ourselves! Taylor just gave me this look—you know, the one—and went back to work like nothing had happened. But the Boers? They nearly lost it, trying to stifle their laughter. One of them hissed, 'Pasop, jy sal die rotte wegjaag!'"

"What does that mean?" another runner asked, grinning.

"Careful, you'll scare off the rats." The absurdity of the moment brought another round of laughter from the runners. For a moment, the grim reality of the siege seemed to dissolve in the humour of Tau's story.

"But then," Tau continued, his voice steadying as he brought them back to the moment, "it was like they remembered where they were. They went quiet, and we knew we had to move fast."

The laughter faded, the group leaning in closer again.

"We finished placing the charges, but just as we were about to retreat, one of their patrols must've heard something. Maybe the scrape of a boot, maybe nothing at all. Either way, they started shouting, and that was it. We had to run."

"And the explosion?" one of the older runners asked.

Tau's lips twitched into a faint grin. "The whole sky lit up. The kiln didn't just go—it blew apart like a thunderstorm. You could hear the Boers scrambling, shouting over each other. That sniper post is gone now. No more sharpshooters picking off our men."

The runners murmured in awe, their voices overlapping as they dissected the story. Pasha stayed quiet, letting the scene unfold in his mind. He could almost hear the crack of the rifles, feel the tension of crouching in the gully, and see the bright flash of the explosion lighting up the night.

"And Taylor?" someone asked. "What did he do after?"

"Didn't even look back. Just said, 'That'll do,' and started walking back toward the trenches. Cool as ice, that one."

The group burst into laughter again, their camaraderie a balm against the siege's ever-present weight. Even Pasha couldn't help but smile, though his thoughts lingered on the courage it took to face danger so calmly.

"You'll get your chance, Liffey," one of the runners said, catching Pasha's contemplative expression. "Stick with us long enough, and you'll have your own story."

The others nodded in agreement, their voices low but warm. For the first time since his arrival in Mafeking, Pasha felt something like belonging. He wasn't a hero, but he was part of something bigger—a web of shared purpose that stretched from the runners on the stoep to the defenders in the trenches.

The faint rumble of artillery broke the stillness, reminding them that the siege was never far away. The group began to stir, standing and stretching as the day's work called them back to action. Pasha adjusted the pouch slung over his shoulder and followed them toward the post office, the shadows of the acacia tree shifting behind him.

The story of the Brickfields would stay with him, not just as a tale of heroism but as a reminder of what this siege demanded of everyone—runners, defenders, and soldiers alike. Whatever came next, Pasha knew, would carry its weight. For now, he was glad to listen and to learn.

THE LAST SALUTE

March 5, 1900.

The coffin rested in the centre of the yard, draped in a fresh Union Jack flag. No bugles. No fanfare. Just the steady scrape of boots on dry earth as soldiers took their places in silence. The sun, unrelenting, cast sharp shadows across the ground, but no one shifted to seek shade. This was not the time for comfort.

Sergeant Major William Ashton Taylor was gone.

Pasha stood at the back, hands clasped, shoulders stiff. The siege had hardened them all, but this loss felt different. Taylor had been more than a soldier—he had been a presence, a man who led with quiet authority, who stood firm when everything around them crumbled. The men in the front rows had fought beside him. Some owed him their lives. Now, they stood with bowed heads, their uniforms threadbare, their faces hollowed by hunger and war.

Colonel Baden-Powell was among them, an unusual sight at a funeral like this. It was whispered among the ranks that no British officer had ever attended the burial of a man like Taylor—a man of colour, a man who, despite his rank, had always been kept on the edges of history. But here, in Mafeking, the siege had erased those lines. Taylor had proved himself beyond question, and even the rigid rules of empire had been forced to yield.

Pasha's eyes lingered on the coffin, on the rough-hewn wood, hastily nailed together, another cruel reminder of how war stripped everything to necessity. Taylor had fought at the Brickfields, held the line when the Boers threatened to break through. He had given orders with unwavering resolve, even as "Au Sanna," the Boer artillery gun, thundered from across the valley. The shell had landed close—too close. By the time Pasha reached him, the dust had already begun to settle. The damage was done.

The chaplain stepped forward, clearing his throat, his voice steady despite the grief weighing the air. "We commend to Almighty God the soul of William Ashton Taylor, a soldier of His Majesty's forces, who gave his life to defend this town and its people. He was a man of great courage, a servant of peace in times of war, and a friend to all who knew him."

Pasha listened, but his mind drifted. He thought of the story Tau had told, the last mission Taylor had led. The Brickfields, the sniper's post, the explosion that had ripped through the night. He had laughed with the others at the absurdity of the moment— the misfiring of a sniper's joke, the ridiculousness of war allowing for something so human as laughter—but the cost had been real. Taylor had fought for a country that had never truly called him its own, and yet here he lay, honoured by those who had marched beside him.

The final words of the service faded, replaced by the crack of rifle fire—a last salute. The shots rang out, sharp and final, echoing beyond the town walls.

Baden-Powell stepped forward, his movements measured, his face unreadable. He touched the coffin, fingers curling slightly against the flag-draped wood. Then, in a moment that would be remembered long after the siege was over, he raised his hand in salute. It was brief, but it was enough.

The soldiers lowered the coffin into the ground, their movements slow, deliberate. Pasha swallowed hard, his throat tight. He had known Taylor only briefly, but in those moments, he had seen the measure of the man. The siege had taken many already, and it would take more before it was over. But some losses cut deeper.

The first shovelful of earth hit the coffin lid with a dull thud. Then another. And another.

Pasha stepped back. The sky was wide and cloudless, the sun bright, but the world felt dimmer without Taylor's presence.

A crow wheeled overhead, its black wings cutting across the light. It dipped once, casting a fleeting shadow over the grave before vanishing beyond the walls of Mafeking.

Pasha watched it go, knowing the siege would ask more of them before it was done. But today, they had lost one of their best.

And war would not pause to grieve.

THE COST OF HUNGER

March 29, 1900

The wooden window shutters of the Mafeking post office clattered softly in the warm breeze, the only sound against the stillness of the dusty yard.

The thorn trees in the courtyard stretched overhead, their branches casting spindly shadows across the dry earth. Pasha sat beneath one of them, his back pressed against the rough bark, a spot of shade in the sweltering heat. His muscles tensed, his eyes following the scene unfolding before him.

A desk and chairs had been dragged outside, forming a rough, open-air courtroom. Edward Cecil, dressed in a neatly pressed khaki uniform, sat at the centre, commanding the scene with cold authority. His black armband stood against the crisp fabric, a solemn reminder of those lost to the Boer bombardments. As Baden-Powell's Chief of Staff, Cecil carried the total weight of the Empire in every decision he made today.

Next to him, Charles Bell, the magistrate of Mafeking District, sat awkwardly in his chair. He dabbed at his forehead with a handkerchief, his role here reduced to that of a witness under martial law. He had no say or authority to intervene, and the knowledge weighed visibly on him.

But it was Sol Plaatje who commanded Pasha's attention. Sol stood just a few feet from the desk, his posture straight, hands on his hips, his face a mask of quiet concentration. He spoke softly, translating the charges—theft of livestock during

126

wartime—his voice clear but devoid of emotion. Pasha could see the weight on him. Sol was more than just a translator; he was a man torn between two worlds. A native son, but one bound by duty to the Empire, forced to speak the words of those who ruled, even as his heart lay with the people.

Pasha watched him closely, understanding the complexity of the man standing before him. Sol was the bridge, connecting two worlds that seemed eternally at odds. His eyes flickered briefly toward Jan Malhombe, the accused. For a split second, the struggle was visible on his face. How do you voice injustice when you are bound by your role to the system perpetuating it?

Jan Malhombe, the Zulu farm labourer, stood tall, his expression fixed and unwavering. He'd taken a goat to feed himself during the long siege, so the Empire demanded his life. The cold and unyielding law of the British had no room for hunger, no room for desperation.

Sol's voice faltered, only for a moment, but he regained his composure. The words flowed, but the conflict was beneath the surface—a man torn between duty and truth. Pasha could see the weight of responsibility that sat heavy on Sol's shoulders, a man who translated the language of power but carried the burden of his people's suffering.

Across from Sol, Chief Melemo of the Barolong stood, silent, his arms crossed, watching with tight-lipped frustration. Brought in to observe, his presence did nothing to change the outcome. Pasha could feel the tension between the men—the futility of Melemo's role as a witness in a trial where his voice would never matter.

"Theft of livestock during wartime is punishable by death," Cecil said flatly, his voice cutting through the air. Sol translated it though his eyes remained on Jan. Though steady, his words were heavy with the knowledge that this trial was not about justice but control.

The defence attorney, J.W. de Kock, muttered something about hunger and the siege, but his voice was drowned in the heat. The argument was empty, a half-hearted defence against an imperial machine that would not be swayed by hunger or need.

"Jan Malhombe, you are sentenced to death. Execution by firing squad. Two days." Cecil's words fell like stones into the silent yard.

Sol translated, his voice quieter now, the internal battle playing out in the subtle tightness of his jaw. He could not change the outcome. He could only deliver the message—words of death in a language meant to oppress.

Above them, a black crow sat motionless on the branch of the thorn tree, its wings folded neatly, its eyes gleaming in the light. The bird did not move, watching the scene below - a silent witness, as still as the men standing beneath it.

The crowd began to stir, whispers passing among the soldiers and townsfolk. Sergeant Heald moved forward, placing a firm hand on Jan's arm, preparing to lead him away. De Kock muttered something in Jan's ear, but the condemned man didn't respond. His fate had already been sealed.

Pasha sat still though his mind raced. He watched Sol, watched the silent tension in his every movement. There was no victory here, no justice. Sol's role in this trial had been to speak the coloniser's words, but Pasha knew that deep inside, Sol carried the burden of knowing he could do nothing to stop it.

The black crow shifted on the branch above, its feathers rustling in the warm breeze. The trial had ended, and the verdict passed, but Pasha could feel the weight of it all—the burden of being powerless in the face of an unrelenting force.

As the crowd dispersed, Pasha remained sitting, watching the scene dissolve before him. The crow remained in its dark form, a shadow against the sinking sun, a silent observer, much like Pasha himself—caught between worlds, watching as the Empire passed judgment on men like Jan.

THE LAST HOUR

April 2 5:30 p.m.

The last light of day fled Mafeking, forging long shadows on the silent buildings. The town felt heavy as if even the air understood what would happen. Pasha sat with the other runners in the post office courtyard, their backs against the cool stone wall, shaded. The usual chatter was absent, replaced by a sombre stillness.

Sol Plaatje stood before them. His voice was steady, soft yet firm. The runners listened closely as he detailed the next day's routes; they would leave Mafeking under the cape of darkness. His words were deliberate, as though he knew the evening carried more than routine tasks. Something unspoken lingered in the air, casting a shadow over their usual work.

Jan Malhombe, the Zulu farm labourer, stood a few yards away. His execution was set for the early evening, just outside the town hall, within sight of the runners. Jan's crime—stealing a goat during the long siege—had been born of hunger and desperation. However, under martial law, survival wasn't a defence. In this town, held tight by siege and fear, the law had no room for leniency. There would be no reprieve.

As Sol's voice droned on, assigning final routes, Pasha's gaze drifted toward the far end of the yard where the preparations for the execution had already begun. The soldiers had formed a line, rifles at their sides. The weight of it settled in Pasha's chest—he had seen death before. Still, the weight of an execution gnawed at him in a way that battle never could. There was a finality to it, a silence that followed death's hammer blow. Pasha had felt it before, but this—this was different. It clung to the air like a storm.

As Sol finished speaking, a sudden stillness took hold. The wind died, and the sounds of the town faded; every second felt like it was about to crack. The runners sat, rigid and alert, their eyes drawn to the courtyard, to the source of the tension hanging between them all.

And then it came—the commands, crisp and devoid of hesitation, cutting through the heavy air:

"Ready!"

The runners tensed, their bodies stiff against the cold stone wall.

"Aim!"

Pasha's breath caught, his eyes fixed on nothing but the dust rising faintly in the courtyard.

"Fire!"

The sharp crack of rifle fire followed, shattering the stillness. The shots echoed through the streets, bouncing off stone walls and filling the space where silence had once been. Pasha flinched, just as the others did, but none of them moved. They didn't need to. They knew exactly what had just happened. Jan was dead.

For a moment, everything stood still. Time seemed to pause, hanging in the air like the smoke from the rifles. Pasha's heart pounded, his chest tight as the finality of it hit him. He struggled to grasp it, the way life could be taken so swiftly, so coldly, with nothing more than the pull of a trigger. Jan had been alive only moments ago, standing in the same town as them, breathing the same air, and now… gone. The world kept turning, but it felt like something important had been lost, swept away by the sound of the shots.

Sol's voice was quieter now, as though even he felt the weight of what had just happened. "You know your duties. Stay sharp."

The runners began to stir. There was no rush, no urgency. The sound of the shots had drained the group's normal energy. They dispersed, heading off to their tasks, but the usual ease was gone.

Pasha lingered his eyes following the path to the town hall where Jan had been taken. The smoke from the gunfire still seemed to hang in the air, a visible reminder of the empire's power—cold, efficient, and absolute. He felt the fire of anger in his chest, but it was a fire with no outlet, no place to go. There was nothing he could do.

With a deep breath, Pasha stood and prepared himself. He had messages to collect and deliver tomorrow—just like every day. But today felt different. Jan's execution was a reminder of how precarious their lives were under the Empire's rule. The shots echoed in his mind long after the sound had faded.

BETWEEN SHADOWS
AND STORIES

The clank-clank of the Columbian press echoed through the courtyard, steady as a heartbeat. Inside the Mafeking Mail, ink-stained hands wrestled with the groaning machinery, coaxing another edition into existence.

Pasha sat outside on the warm step, one leg stretched out, the other bent at the knee, arms resting loosely. The air smelled of fresh paper and dust, curling in the afternoon heat. He wasn't part of the press, but he felt close enough to its pulse—watching, listening, straddling two worlds.

Inside, George N.H. Whales barked orders, his voice rising over the mechanical rhythm, while Glover, the printer, grumbled at the press like a man scolding an old mule. The newsroom was a battlefield of ink and urgency, a place where stories were shaped before they reached the world beyond the siege.

Lady Sarah Wilson passed through the square, her presence unhurried but deliberate. She was the first female war correspondent of the Boer War and the aunt of Winston Churchill—a connection that lent her articles weight. She always nodded to the runners. Just a small gesture, but in a town where messengers lived and died by their orders, it meant something.

But it was Vere Stent who fascinated Pasha most. The Reuters correspondent moved with restless energy, a cigarette dangling from his lips, his eyes always scanning, always calculating. He asked questions that made casual conversation feel like an interrogation.

"What was it like, Pasha?" Vere asked one afternoon, leaning against the step beside him. *"London, the crowds, the lions... must've been quite a sight."*

Pasha grinned, eyes drifting toward the horizon, letting the memory wash over him. Earl's Court. The sheer spectacle of it— the warriors, the reenactments, the sea of white faces watching from the stands. *"London's a show,"* he murmured. *"The biggest one of all. They watched us like we were no different from the animals. But we played our part."*

From the shadows, Ewan Ravenscroft—the journalist they called "the man with the hat"—sat with his wide-brimmed hat tipped forward, listening. He had been in that audience at Savage South Africa, watching the same battles play out as performance, each warrior carefully placed for maximum effect. He had seen Pasha then, though he said nothing now. His amusement was subtle—a twitch of his lips, an exhale that might have been a laugh.

There was something about Ravenscroft that set him apart from the others. He rarely spoke, but his journal was always open, scribbled notes disappearing into its pages. His gaze lingered on things the others overlooked. Pasha couldn't shake the feeling that Ravenscroft saw through him—as if their stories were cut from the same fabric, though neither knew quite how.

The courtyard hummed with movement. Angus Hamilton of *The Times* strode by, his booming voice carrying above the din, while quieter figures from *The Morning Post* shuffled in his wake. The siege had turned the post office into the heart of Mafeking's press, a place where war was shaped into words.

Pasha listened, letting their conversations drift around him. He was not a journalist. His story would never grace their pages. Yet, here he sat, among the voices that decided how history would remember this war.

As the sun dipped, the journalists gathered their notes and drifted toward Dixon's Hotel, where drinks would loosen their tongues. Vere lingered, sharing a cigarette with Pasha. They smoked in silence, the distant rumble of gunfire barely registering.

"You know," Vere mused, watching the smoke curl. *"I'd trade all these stories for one day in London, watching that show with you. Sounds like something the world ought to know more about."*

Pasha didn't reply. He didn't need to. The weight of it hung between them, the unspoken understanding that some stories never made it to print.

As the last press run fell silent, the courtyard emptied.

Pasha remained, watching the world move around him, never quite inside it. The war had given him purpose, but it had not given him a voice. His story was never written—only lived.

From the far side of the courtyard, Ewan Ravenscroft turned a page in his weathered notebook. He had seen enough men slip between the cracks of history to recognize when one was worth remembering.

He had watched Pasha Liffey since the moment he arrived in Mafeking, not just because of the boy's quiet resilience, but because history had a way of leaving men like him in the margins.

Ravenscroft exhaled slowly, rolling his pencil between his fingers. He had sat in the grandstands of Earl's Court, watched Savage South Africa unfold with all its orchestrated spectacle. He had seen Pasha back then, the warrior reduced to theatre, the savage dressed for applause.

Yet here he was now, moving through the heart of an actual war—not in costume, not in performance, but in reality. The irony sat heavy in Ravenscroft's gut. No one would write about Pasha. Not in the dispatches, not in the war reports. Not unless someone made sure they did.

He studied Pasha one last time, the way he sat—half in shadow, half in light. He would not approach him yet. Some stories could not be forced; they had to unfold.

Instead, he flipped to a fresh page. Without hesitation, he scrawled a single line across the top:

"The Unwritten History of Pasha Liffey."

The ink dried fast in the warm air.

Tomorrow, the world would go on. The press would print its stories. The war would move forward.

And somewhere between the lines, so would Pasha Liffey.

VALLEY OF DEATH

May 10, 1900

The clusters of tents along the kopjes between the Boer artillery positions flapped like dying birds in the wind.

At an observation post west of Jackal Tree Hill, beneath a makeshift canopy, a group of Boers sat around a small fire, coffee brewing, their Mauser rifles resting on the ground, ready to be picked up at a moment's notice. The Boers were rough men, hard-edged and worn from months of fighting.

Below them, dry streambeds cut through the parched earth, joining a dry riverbed—a hollow scar across the land, a reminder of the driest season in years. The sun was rising, bleeding slivers of light onto the landscape below.

The lookout, thin as a rake with an enormous red beard, spotted movement in the valley below. He raised his binoculars, and there, at the edge of his vision, he saw a lone figure running toward Mafeking, a shadow flickering along the dry riverbed.

"Daar!" he screeched, his voice sharp and guttural, his Mauser pointing toward the runner. "Daar, die fokken kaffir! Skiet hom!" - Shoot the runner!

The men scrambled for their Mausers, their fingers steady on the triggers as they lined up their sights on the fleeting figure of Pasha.

The dry, cracked earth bit into his bare feet as Pasha sprinted along the riverbed, his breaths coming in quick, jagged bursts.

With each step, gritty sand churned beneath him, sharp little stones pressing into his soles. This riverbed had once carried life, but now it lay abandoned, a blistered vein beneath the unforgiving sun.

Ahead of him, an anthill rose like a sentinel on the riverbank. He threw himself behind it, pressing close to the ground, his chest heaving. Bullets tore into the anthill, spraying red earth into the air. The impact sent tremors through the ground beneath him. Pasha clenched the dirt in his hands, sinking lower, willing himself to vanish into the earth. The sun was rising – giving its last kiss to the horizon.

Pasha sat motionless against the anthill, his chest rising and falling in quick, shallow breaths. Far away, the Boers shouted to one another, their garbled voices carried faintly on the wind, laced with frustration—the echoes of rifle shots dissolved into the stillness of the riverbed.

The pounding of blood in his ears was deafening, a relentless drumbeat that anchored him to the moment. The world around him felt unreal, blurred by exhaustion and adrenaline, but his mind stayed sharp, calculating his next move. He forced himself to remain motionless, every second stretching out into eternity, his heart hammering against the hard ground.

When the barrage ceased, Pasha's instincts screamed at him to run, to move before the Boer snipers adjusted their sights. Summoning his strength, he burst from cover, legs pumping, each step a prayer for survival. The Mausers barked again, but Pasha was already out of range, a shadow flickering across the dry riverbed, swallowed by the vastness of the terrain.

As the town's edge came into view, Pasha slowed to a walk. His bare feet brushed against the rough, dusty ground of Main Street as he neared the post office. The street buzz faded as he crossed the threshold and entered the office, the weight of his mission pressing heavily on his shoulders.

Inside, Sol Plaatje looked up from his desk, meeting Pasha's gaze. In that brief moment, the urgency passed between them without a word. Pasha reached beneath his shirt, drawing out the sealed envelope hidden against his skin. His fingers trembled as he handed it over.

Sol's eyes flicked over the envelope, then widened as he broke the seal and scanned the contents. His expression shifted—a flicker of something rare and fragile in a besieged town: hope.

"The column is coming," Sol said softly, his voice just loud enough for Pasha to hear. "Relief is on its way."

Pasha slumped into the nearest chair, his body finally surrendering to exhaustion. The weight he had carried—both the message and the knowledge of its importance—seemed to lift, if only slightly. Around them, the press office remained a hive of quiet activity, the clanking of the Columbian press now a steady undercurrent to the moment's significance.

From the corner of the room, the journalist with the wide-brimmed hat watched intently. His notebook lay open on his lap, but his pen was still, his gaze fixed on Pasha. The shadow of his hat hid his expression. Still, there was a sharpness to his presence as if he were committing every detail to memory.

History was being made, and the man with the hat was already shaping how it would be told.

Above Mafeking, where Boer tents flapped like dying birds in the dry wind, a crow tumbled from the dusky sky, flick-flacking through the fading light like a shadow of things yet to come.

THEATRE OF WAR

In Nottingham, an effigy of Paul Kruger, complete with his trademark top hat, was hoisted up a lamppost. The rope creaked as the wind tugged it gently back and forth, its stiff figure swaying like a condemned man. Below, a sea of University College students erupted into cheers, their exuberance unrestrained as the effigy symbolised, in their minds, the Boer leader's defeat and the empire's inevitable triumph.

At the centre of the square, a young man proudly dressed as Colonel Baden-Powell paraded in full khaki, saluting the crowd with the exaggerated fervour of an actor playing to a packed house. Around him, his peers waved Union Jacks and belted patriotic songs until their voices cracked, their faces flushed with revelry. Every corner of the square pulsed with noise—fireworks cracked overhead, bonfires flickered in the gathering dusk, and laughter echoed against the brick facades. The air seemed alive, electric with the unearned fervour of a victory claimed from afar.

One student had climbed astride a crude replica of "Long Tom," the infamous Boer cannon that had haunted British troops throughout the siege. His friends gathered around, barking out commands and mimicking battlefield strategies, their play-acting accompanied by wild cheers from the crowd. It was chaos—pure, unbridled celebration, a vindication of British might that no one here had earned, but everyone claimed as their own.

The news of Mafeking's relief had hit Britain like a thunderclap. At precisely 9:35 p.m. on May 18, 1900, an excited footman burst into the Mansion House in London to deliver the announcement, igniting instant celebration. What began as a ripple of excited whispers spread like wildfire across the nation. When the news reached Nottingham, the streets were already teeming with revellers. Effigies of Kruger and other Boer leaders hung from lampposts like trophies of war.

Nottingham was similar to the rest of the Empire that night. Fireworks and bonfires illuminated streets from Manchester to Glasgow, London to Bristol. Across the globe, in the far reaches of the Empire, cities like Toronto, Sydney, Melbourne, and Auckland erupted in similar fervour. Union Jacks waved, patriotic anthems filled the air, and fireworks lit up distant skies. The term "mafficking" had already begun to circulate, coined to capture this precise moment of wild, unrestrained jubilation.

In the pubs and halls of Nottingham, men raised their glasses to Baden-Powell and the brave souls who had endured the 217-day siege. Few paused to think about what it must have been like— trapped inside Mafeking, surviving on the slimmest of rations, facing death daily. For most here, the siege was not a tale of suffering but a heroic story; its relief was a vindication of British superiority.

In the heart of the square, a group of students had rigged up a crude stage. A mock Queen Victoria—played by one of their peers draped in a bedsheet crown—waved graciously to the crowd, prompting more laughter and cheers. They celebrated the relief of Mafeking and the Empire, the unshakable belief in British resolve and dominance.

And yet, beneath the laughter and firelight, a quieter truth flickered like the dying embers of a bonfire. While Nottingham and Piccadilly Circus roared with patriotic fervour, the people of Mafikeng—the Tshidi Barolong—remained silent. For them, the relief was not a triumph but a means of survival. They had endured the siege alongside their British allies, suffering just as great, yet their voices were absent from the Empire's grand narrative. Their silence was drowned out by the noise of fireworks and the crackling flames of Kruger's effigy.

The effigy swayed in the firelight, its edges charred as the flames consumed its form, a haunting echo of the Empire's need to vilify and conquer. To the crowd, it was a symbol, a scapegoat to burn and cheer over. But to those watching closely, it was a reminder of how history is shaped—by the stories that survive and those that are swallowed by the smoke.

As the bonfires burned low and the streets emptied, the echoes of "mafficking" lingered across the land. For the British Empire, the relief of Mafeking was not just a victory but a reaffirmation of its might, which would resonate long after the cheers had faded into the night.

CROSSROADS IN THE DUST

After 217 days of relentless bombardment, gnawing hunger, and the suffocating grip of fear, Mafeking erupted into unrestrained celebration. The siege was over.

The British flag, tattered and torn by the violence of war, fluttered stubbornly above the ruins—a battered but unyielding symbol of defiance. Its fabric waved over the town like a survivor's battle cry.

As the news of relief spread, the once-silent streets surged with life. Gaunt residents spilt out of their homes, their voices rising like a flood breaking its dam. Shouts of triumph ricocheted off crumbling walls and empty buildings. Children, who had spent months confined by fear, now raced barefoot through the dusty streets, their laughter cutting through the still air like a song of defiance. This was a victory—raw, unrefined, and almost feral.

For Pasha, the moment felt both monumental and strangely hollow. He stood apart from the throng, his dark eyes scanning the revelry with quiet detachment. His survival, though celebrated by the crowd, felt different—a solitary triumph amidst the communal joy. The weight of his role as a runner lingered within him, pressing down like the oppressive heat that still clung to the air.

Across the square, Ewan Ravenscroft leaned against the broken frame of a building, his wide-brimmed hat shading his face. The journalist was a shadowed figure, his notebook on his knee, pencil flicking quietly. Ravenscroft had arrived in Mafeking days before the siege. Now, he watched the celebration with his usual calm, capturing every nuance for readers far removed from this dusty town. His pencil slowed as his gaze landed on Pasha, standing like a silent observer amidst the chaos. There was something about the young man—his posture, the haunted look in his eyes—that Ravenscroft couldn't ignore. The story here wasn't just the siege's end but the stories of men like Pasha who had survived it. For now, though, the journalist kept his thoughts to himself.

Pasha's attention shifted as a rider approached, weaving through the throng. The officer dismounted fluidly, his polished boots striking the dry earth. Pasha's breath caught. He knew that figure—how he carried himself with a quiet authority. It was Douglas Henry Fraser—the man who had once taken Pasha, as a boy, from Mafeking to England.

Pasha hesitated, then stepped forward, threading his way through the crowd until he stood within arm's reach. "Mister Fraser."

Fraser turned, his brow furrowing until recognition dawned. His face softened into a rare smile. "Liffey? Is that you?" He stepped closer, studying the lean figure before him.

"It's me … Pasha", the faintest smile tugging at his lips.

Fraser nodded, his gaze momentarily distant as if tracing their shared past. "It's been at least two years. What are you doing here?"

"I've been a runner. I brought the message from Mahon to the town."

Fraser's eyes widened. His hand instinctively reached for his hat, which he pushed back as he shook his head in disbelief. "You were the runner? Through the Boer lines?" He exhaled sharply, a mix of admiration and astonishment flickering across his face. "That's no small thing, Liffey. No small thing at all."

They stood silently for a moment, the crowd's noise fading into the background. Fraser's voice was quieter now, almost reflective. "I'm heading back to England soon. If you're interested in returning, I'll pay your fare. You've earned that much and more."

The offer hung in the air, laden with possibilities. Pasha met Fraser's gaze, the weight of his words settling on him like a tangible force. England. The place he had left behind. The place that now called to him like a siren's song. He had dreamed of returning, and here was the opportunity, handed to him by the man who had first taken him there all those years ago.

Around them, the celebration continued unabated. The townspeople danced and sang, their joy unchecked by the gauntness of their faces or the emptiness of their stores. The Union Jack fluttered above, a symbol of survival and resilience. Yet, to Pasha, it was also a reminder of his journey—from the dusty streets of Mafeking to the stages of London and back again. It was a journey that had shaped him, forged him in the fires of war and spectacle, and left him yearning for something he could not yet name.

Above him, a crow dipped and soared into the gathering twilight, its dark wings cutting through the fading light. Its flight traced an invisible line between the past and what lay ahead, a silent reminder that survival was not the end of the journey but the beginning of another chapter.

And so, as Mafeking roared with triumph, Pasha prepared for what lay beyond. He did not know the future but knew one thing: he would not stand still. The allure of England, adventure, and the promise of a new story called.

THE JOURNEY NORTH

The ship's horn split the damp air as England loomed ahead. Pasha stood at the railing, his fingers curled tight over the iron rail. The last time he had arrived on these shores, he was a curiosity—a performer in a grand imperial spectacle. Now, he returned a soldier, a survivor. But had anything really changed?

London greeted him with its usual cacophony. Carriages clattered over cobblestones, street vendors hawked their wares, and a sea of humanity bustled through the station as if the war and its horrors were a distant echo. Pasha moved through the crowds, his senses alive with the city's pulse. Yet beneath its surface was a tension he hadn't expected.

Pasha got sucked into a crowd heading to Trafalgar Square, where the throng thickened. The square was packed—thousands spilling onto its cobbles, banners raised high above the sea of heads. "No More Bloodshed!" and "End This War!" proclaimed the slogans, defiant in their simplicity. The voices of dissent surged and swayed like a tide, their energy palpable.

Drawn by the fervour, Pasha edged closer to the crowd's heart. A makeshift stage had been erected, and one speaker after another climbed it, their voices rising above the din.

"War is not the answer!" thundered a man with a booming voice. "Our brothers are dying while those in power count their gold!"

The crowd roared its agreement, their cheers echoing off the statues and buildings that framed the square. The air crackled with urgency, and for a moment, Pasha felt swept up in it—a current of anger and hope colliding.

A woman took the stage, her presence magnetic. "Unity is our strength!" she cried, her voice piercing the noise. "We must come together to demand peace! Enough blood has been spilled!"

The crowd's response was deafening, their cheers filling the space like a living thing. Pasha lingered at the edge, observing but not engaging. These voices were powerful, their passion undeniable, but he felt like an outsider peering into a world he could not grasp.

Turning to a man standing nearby, Pasha raised his voice above the commotion. "Excuse me, have you heard of "Savage South Africa"?"

The man, his cap pulled low against the evening chill, looked up, his expression impatient. "Aye, it's in Manchester now. It's been there since June. Drawing crowds like nothing else."

Pasha nodded, though his thoughts raced ahead. Manchester— farther than he had hoped, but it was where he needed to go.

The train north carried him through a countryside heavy with summer, the green fields and smoke-streaked skies a stark contrast to the arid plains of Mafeking. By the time he reached Manchester, the city hummed with industry. Its streets pulsed with the rhythm of factories, workers' faces etched with exhaustion.

Finding "Savage South Africa" at Broughton Rangers Football Club was simple. The banners marking its entrance were bold and bright, boasting re-enactments of the Boer War's latest battles. The show had adapted and been revitalised to mirror the very conflict Pasha had survived. It was the last week of July.

The crowd outside was electric, eager for the spectacle promised within. But Pasha did not join them. Instead, he moved purposefully through the gates, his eyes scanning the bustling activity of the showground.

Inside, the air was thick with the earthy scent of animal dung and damp mud, the ground churned by the heavy footfall of performers and workers alike. Performers moved with practised efficiency, preparing for the evening's show. Pasha's heart quickened as he spotted a familiar figure near the animal enclosures.

"Jack!" Pasha called, his voice cutting through the din, steady but guarded.

Texas Jack turned slowly, his broad hat tilting just enough to cast his face in shadow. His expression sharpened as his eyes found Pasha, narrowing with recognition. The usual bravado— a grin or some quick-witted remark—was absent. Instead, there was something harder in his gaze, something unreadable. For a moment, neither man moved.

"Mr. Jack," Pasha said, closing the distance with deliberate steps.

Jack's stance shifted slightly, one hand resting on the rail of the enclosure. His presence loomed, commanding, as if every inch

150

of the showground bent to his will. Pasha felt the weight of that reputation—the hard-handed taskmaster. This man wielded control with a sharp tongue and little patience.

There had always been an edge between them, an unspoken tension that flared now in Jack's assessing silence. Pasha stood tall, meeting his gaze, though the space between them felt charged, bristling with unsaid words.

Jack's eyes flicked over him, lingering just long enough to unsettle. "What're you after?" His tone was low, measured, almost dismissive.

Pasha hesitated, the air thick with the past they shared—moments of friction, veiled insults wrapped in the guise of showmanship. He steadied himself. "I want to perform again."

Jack's gaze roamed over Pasha with the precision of a man appraising a piece of equipment, looking for flaws. He leaned against the enclosure, his fingers tapping an uneven rhythm on the wooden rail. The silence between them stretched taut.

The memory of Mafeking hung heavy in Pasha's chest, but he kept his words measured. "I came straight from Mafeking. I was a runner, carrying messages under fire."

At that, Jack's fingers stilled. His eyes flickered briefly—not with surprise, but with something close to grudging respect. He straightened, his expression hard to read. "Mafeking," he repeated, almost to himself, before letting out a faint, humourless chuckle.

There was no acknowledgement, no camaraderie, only the faintest nod as if Jack were filing the information away. Whatever thoughts ran through his mind, they didn't show.

Finally, Jack stepped back, gesturing loosely toward the showground. Back from the wars, eh?" Jack drawled, gaze raking over Pasha. "Think that makes you a star? Think again. You're in, but don't expect me to roll out a welcome mat."

Pasha nodded, his jaw tightening. Jack's approval came laced with conditions, as it always had, but there was no mistaking the opportunity. He turned to go, the weight of the exchange settling in his chest. Behind him, Jack's presence lingered like a shadow, a reminder that nothing here would come freely.

As the evening settled over Manchester, the air heavy with the mingling scents of the showground, Pasha walked the arena's perimeter. Memories of Earl's Court flickered through his mind—of roaring crowds, the crackle of applause, and the thrill of performance. This was different, rougher, yet no less vital. Manchester's smoke-streaked skies lent the show a grittier edge, the glamour of London replaced by a raw determination to entertain.

At the north stand of the football ground, Pasha spotted a familiar group huddled together, their laughter rising above the din. As he drew closer, faces turned his way, and recognition sparked smiles and shouts of greeting. William Savory and Albert Martin—some of the Cape Boys—were among them, their camaraderie still intact despite the miles and months that had passed.

"Pasha!" Savory called, clapping him on the back. "We thought you were still out there, dodging bullets!"

"Barely made it," Pasha replied with a grin, the warmth of the reunion briefly lifting the weight that had clung to him since Mafeking. They chatted easily, catching up on news of South Africa and the stories from the road.

The mood shifted sharply when Pasha, glancing around the group, asked, "What about the Big Zulu? Jacob Johnson? Is he here?"

The group stilled, a heavy silence dropping over them. Savory's face darkened, and Martin stared hard at the ground. For a moment, nobody spoke. The air felt charged as if they were all bracing for something they didn't want to say.

"You haven't heard?" Savory finally muttered, his voice rough.

Pasha frowned, his chest tightening. "Heard what?"

Savory glanced at Martin before looking back at Pasha, his voice thick with reluctance. "Jacob... he's gone. Two weeks ago. I found him in the river back in Nottingham. Dead."

The words slammed into Pasha like a fist. "The river?" he said, his voice rising. "How? What happened?"

"Drowned," Savory spat, the word like a curse. "That's what they said. Open verdict, the coroner called it. But we all know it stinks."

"Stinks, how?" Pasha demanded, his jaw tight. "What aren't you saying?"

Savory shifted on his feet, his anger barely contained. "You know how Jacob was—he didn't take shit from nobody, especially not Texas Jack. Always standing up, always pushing back. That day, he and Jack had words. Over some stupid game with a gun. Jack threatened him—said he'd knock his 'head off.' Jacob didn't back down, not to Jack, not ever."

Martin cut in, his voice low and sharp. "Two days later, they pulled him out of the river. That's what happened."

Pasha felt a flash of rage, hot and immediate. "And that's it?" he hissed. "That's all they've got. Drowned?"

Savory's mouth twisted into a bitter line. "That's what they want us to believe. But Jacob wasn't drunk, not that day. He wasn't stupid, either. You know as well as I do—he wouldn't have just wandered into that river. Not without reason."

Martin's voice was quieter, but it carried a hard edge. "You think Jack didn't know what he was doing? Everyone knows how rough he is. Jacob pushed him too far, and now..." He trailed off, shaking his head.

The group fell into a grim silence, the weight of their words hanging heavy in the air. Around them, the distant noise of the showground carried on, oblivious to the bitterness that had settled among them.

Pasha's fists clenched at his sides, his body taut with frustration. Jacob had been more than just a big man with a loud voice— he'd been a fighter who stood up when others stayed silent. Now he was dead, his life reduced to an "open verdict," his story swept aside like dirt under the empire's boot.

Pasha lowered his head, "He didn't deserve that …. Not Jacob."

"No," Savory replied, his tone raw with anger. "But when you stand tall like he did, they're always ready to cut you down."

Pasha looked at the faces around him. The quiet fury in their eyes mirrored his own. Jacob's death wasn't just a loss; it was a reminder of the lines they all walked, the constant balance between defiance and survival.

The sky darkened, the air thick with smoke and the sour tang of burning oil. A crow swooped low over the showground, its wings carving through the twilight. Pasha followed its flight, something cold settling in his gut. He had returned to this world, but the ground beneath him felt more treacherous than ever.

As the group dispersed, Pasha lingered at the edge of the arena. Jacob Johnson's story gnawed at him, a grim reminder of how easily lives could be lost and voices could be silenced.

The show had always been a place of spectacle, a performance to entertain the masses. But a darker truth lay beneath the bright lights and roaring crowds—one Pasha could no longer ignore.

His story was far from over, and whatever lay ahead, he knew he would find a way to make it his own.

THE FRACTURES BEGIN

The air in Manchester was thick with smoke and rain, clinging to the city's stone streets like a second skin. The town hummed with life, yet every corner seemed cloaked in hostility for Pasha. "Savage South Africa", still a draw for crowds at the Broughton Rangers Football Club, had changed. Beneath its facade of spectacle, the fractures were impossible to ignore.

The performers—Boers, Africans, and Britons—moved like strangers. The camaraderie Pasha once relied on had faded. The Cape Boys, a lively bunch, now whispered amongst themselves, their laughter replaced by wary glances. The Boers, always aloof, had grown bolder in their disdain. Even Texas Jack, whose voice once rallied the camp like a bugle call, barked his commands with an edge that sliced through the already brittle atmosphere.

Outside the camp, Manchester's cobbled streets were no kinder. Children jeered as the performers walked past, their taunts spiked with venom. Pub doors slammed shut when Black faces approached, and when they did not, there was always a man eager to make his prejudice known with a slur or a swing of his fist.

For Pasha, it was a slow boil, a constant pressure that threatened to crack his fragile veneer of control over his anger. But the boil reached its tipping point on a damp Monday night in Lower Broughton.

It began like any other evening. The performers, eager for a reprieve from the grinding monotony of the showground, sought solace in the nearby pubs. Among them was Richard Hill, one of the Cape Boys—a towering figure with a sharp tongue and a quicker temper. The group was drinking, their laughter cutting through the low murmur of the pub as they swapped stories.

But something in the air shifted. A group of white locals began throwing glances, muttering under their breath until one of them, emboldened by drink, approached. The words that followed were not loud but sharp enough to cut through the pub's haze.

When the fight spilt into the street, there was no turning back. Sticks were raised, fists flew, and belts cracked like whips in the chill night air. Shouting echoed down Lower Broughton Road, pulling bystanders into the chaos. Amid the fray, Hill took a blade to the chest, the knife sinking dangerously close to his lung. Blood. So much blood.
Hill stumbled, hands clutching his chest, his breath coming in sharp gasps.
Pasha felt something hot rise in his throat—rage, horror, helplessness.
The crowd pressed in, boots scuffing against the cobblestones. A whistle shrieked. The night spun.
Pasha lunged—someone grabbed his arm. "No! Not now!" A voice, distant, urgent.
But all he could see was the red blooming across Hill's chest..

Police whistles shrieked through the night as officers waded into the chaos, their batons flashing under the dim streetlamps. When the dust settled, Hill was rushed to Salford Royal Hospital, his comrades trailing silently behind, their faces grim and their hands clutching sticks.

The camp buzzed with rage the following day as the details trickled back. Two white men, George Loft and Joseph Scott, were arrested. Loft's sneering remark— "I wasn't going to be struck by a lot of niggers"—stung like a slap, a reminder of the daily battles they faced even outside the ring. Scott, less brazen but no less complicit, claimed he had been defending himself from "a horde of Blacks."

For Pasha, the incident was a spark in a long-smouldering fire. He kept his distance but carried the weight of the tension in his silence.

The "Savage South Africa" show left Manchester in mid-July and then toured Blackpool, Liverpool, Leeds, Sunderland, Glasgow, Edinburgh, Dundee, Aberdeen, Newcastle, Middlesborough, Birmingham, Bristol, Belfast, and finally back to Salford Manchester for the final farewell show in September 1901.

"Savage South Africa" had only been one week into the farewell show in Manchester when Pasha, already restless from the undercurrents of hostility, clashed with a Boer performer over a prop misplaced backstage. What began as a sharp exchange escalated into a shouting match. The Boer's words were biting, his disdain thinly veiled. Pasha, his temper honed by months of strain, gave as good as he got.

The argument flowed into the open, drawing the attention of Texas Jack. "Enough!" he roared, his face set like stone. "Liffey, pack your things. I'm not running a circus for troublemakers."

Pasha watched the performers move past him, their eyes averted. The show had lost its hold on him, or maybe he had lost his hold on it. Texas Jack's words echoed in his mind: "*I'm not running a circus for troublemakers.*"
Troublemaker.
The word burned. He had bled for the Empire, carried messages through gunfire, and dodged death in Mafeking. And yet, here he was, discarded like a broken prop.

Pasha exhaled sharply, turning toward the city's grey skyline. Maybe this country had never been meant for him.

And like that, Pasha's second run with "Savage South Africa" ended. As he walked out of the camp for the last time, the shouts of performers and the roar of distant crowds faded into the damp streets of Manchester. Pasha was truly alone for the first time since he had returned to England.

Adrift and desperate for stability, Pasha drifted south to Wilmslow, a quiet town far removed from Manchester's smoke and grime. At the New Inn, he found work as a groom. Edgar Whiting, the landlord, was a portly man with a booming laugh who gave Pasha a chance, seeing in him a hard worker behind the weariness in his eyes.

The job offered a fleeting peace. The rhythm of hooves on cobblestones, the earthy scent of hay, and the routine of tending horses grounded Pasha in a way that the stage never could. For a time, it seemed he might find redemption in the quiet monotony of the stables.

But peace, for Pasha, was always fragile.

On the evening of Monday, September 30, 1901, the fragility cracked. After a week of diligent work, the bottle's siren call became too much. Pasha wandered into a nearby pub, its warm fire and the tang of ale pulling him in. One drink turned into several, and by the time he staggered back to the New Inn, he was a storm ready to break.

The chaos that followed tore through the quiet Wilmslow night. Pasha raged in the inn's common room, his voice rising drunkenly as furniture splintered and bottles shattered. Guests fled, leaving the mess to the innkeeper and the constable, who soon arrived.

PC Finney, known for his no-nonsense demeanour, faced Pasha head-on. The two clashed, Pasha's fists swinging wildly in the flickering light of the gas lamps. Tables overturned, chairs cracked under the weight of their struggle, and it took the combined effort of Finney and several onlookers to finally subdue him.

By the morning of October 4, 1901, Pasha stood in court. His head hung low as Edgar Whiting spoke on his behalf, describing the hardworking groom behind the chaos. Alderman Thompson, the presiding magistrate, was firm but not unkind. Pasha braced himself, half-expecting the gavel to fall harder. "A discharge with caution."

A rush of breath escaped him, but relief did not come. The weight of it all still sat heavily on his chest.

But despite the court's leniency, the shadows clung to Pasha like a second skin. The once-dazzling applause of his past had dimmed, replaced by the quiet despair of lost potential. The New Inn's cobbled lanes and sleepy cottages were no longer a refuge but a reminder of how far he had fallen.

Pasha continued to work at the inn, his days filled with the steady rhythm of stable chores. But the nights were a battlefield. The bottle remained a constant temptation, its promise of oblivion a siren song in the stillness. Each drink pulled him further into the abyss, each misstep a reminder that redemption was a road littered with obstacles he might never overcome.

As the months wore on, the fire within him dimmed. Pasha moved like a ghost through the stables, haunted by the man he had once been. The quiet moments pressed heavy, the voices of old battles and forgotten dreams whispering in his ear. The path ahead stretched like the ocean he had once crossed—vast, uncertain, and shadowed by a past that refused to let go.

THE WEIGHT OF DEFEAT

The poster slapped to the side of the wall of the Blantyre showground did not need gloss to catch a man's attention. In thick, bold letters, it read:

"THIS SATURDAY: JULY 22! BOXING... CAN YOU TAKE ON THE BASUTO BOXER? ALL BETS WELCOME. PRIZE MONEY."

Inside, the makeshift ring trembled under the shuffle of feet and the hum of the crowd. Laughter, jests, and the clink of coins punctuated the air, thick with the smell of stale beer, sweat, and smoke.

Pasha's fists felt heavy, his knuckles raw from the blows he had already thrown. Across the ring, Joseph Smith—a man built like a locomotive, his muscles taut with the strength of a blacksmith—stood with a quiet, dangerous calm. Smith was known to the crowd as a rising star in bare-knuckle boxing, and tonight, he was proving why.

The punch came fast, an uppercut that exploded into Pasha's jaw like a lightning bolt. His world tilted, the edges of his vision darkening as he staggered back, blood filling his mouth, the metallic taste bitter against his tongue. Pasha tried to steady himself, his legs wobbly beneath him. The crowd roared, a mix of cheers and taunts, as Smith advanced, his fists cocked, ready to deliver the final blow.

Pasha managed a weak jab, connecting with Smith's ribs. Still, it was more an act of defiance than any real threat. Smith barely flinched, his eyes locked on Pasha with the cold focus of a predator closing in on its prey.

Smith closed in, his fists a relentless rhythm. Pasha tried to move, to slip away, but the weight of the years pressed down on him—London, the war, the show, the river, the nights lost to drink.

He had fought so many times, in so many places, but never had it felt so futile.

The punch came. He saw it too late. The world snapped sideways.

It was a left hook that slammed into Pasha's temple. His knees buckled, and he hit the canvas with a sickening thud. The crowd erupted, hats tossed in the air as coins changed hands, the excitement palpable in the smoke-filled tent. Pasha blinked up at the ceiling, his body refusing to obey the desperate commands from his brain.

Joseph Smith stood over him, triumphant, his chest heaving from the exertion of the fight. The ringmaster, William Adamson, lifted Smith's arm as the crowd approved. Pasha could hear it, the mixture of admiration and pity that flowed through the spectators. He had lost, but defeat was just another chapter in the story in this brutal world of travelling shows and makeshift rings.

Smith had won, and though he was not yet Scotland's bare-knuckle champion, tonight had proven he was on his way. The year was 1905, and the title would soon be his.

Pasha, still dazed, rolled onto his side and spit blood onto the canvas. His body ached, every breath sending a sharp pain through his ribs. He had been beaten, and there was no denying it. Slowly, with the help of William Forbes—a fellow boxer who had joined the circuit weeks before—Pasha dragged himself to his feet. Forbes handed him a flask, the burn of whisky sharp as Pasha took a long gulp, trying to numb the pain that radiated through his battered body.

"You put up a good fight," Forbes muttered, glancing at the crowd dispersing. "Blantyre next. Then Hamilton. Smith's the favourite now, but you'll get your shot again."

Pasha nodded, wiping the blood from his mouth with his hand. He knew he would be back in the ring soon enough. This was the life he had chosen—no glory without the grit. But tonight, the sting of defeat hung heavy in the air.

The pub was warm and loud, filled with the same rough crowd that had watched the fight. Smith sat at a table, surrounded by admirers, his victory the talk of the night. Pasha sat in a corner with Forbes, nursing another drink. The whisky dulled the edges of his pain, but it could not erase the loss.

Forbes pulled a string of tobacco from his coat, then patted his pockets for his knife; he glanced at Pasha. "Forgot mine. Can I borrow yours?"

Pasha handed him his knife. "Still carrying that knife, I see," Forbes grinned, cutting a tobacco strip. Pasha gave a brief nod, the knife a small but steadying weight in his pocket, a reminder of past fights and future battles.

The night wore on, the pub a blur of laughter, liquor, and slurred stories, till the night's sharp edges softened into a warm haze.

Pasha staggered home, his fingers curled around the penknife, the worn wood smooth against his palm.
It had been with him through war, the ring, and nights where survival had felt more like defiance than fate.
He held onto it now—not as a weapon, but as proof that he was still here.
Tomorrow, the ring would be waiting. And Pasha would fight again.

BLOOD ON THE ROAD

August 11 was no ordinary night in Larkhall. That Friday's old moon shimmered on the railway tracks of Merryton station. In the distance stood Glasgow—its sky filling with smoke from the chimneys of red-brick houses, shrouded in smoke that curled from the chimneys like ghosts whispering tales of toil and trouble. The street-facing walls of the whitewashed cottages surrounding Dykehead Colliery on Summerlee Road blushed in the moonlight.

It was just after nightfall, and where Hamilton Street intersected with Summerlee Road and Carlisle Road, a tangled, overgrown gusset lay choked with weeds and rotting wooden palings. A pony and cart approached the overgrown gusset from the south end of an unlit lane lined by hedgerows—Summerlee Road—groaning under its coal load; wheels crunched over the rough gravel littering the road.

The pony's hooves rang out slowly, a steady clip on the gravel road. At the reins, a young driver—just a slip of a lad—leaned forward, urging the pony along. Just before nine p.m., a group of miners trudged from Merryton Station to the east, their laughter cutting through the haze like a lantern in the gloom, chatting loudly about the day's labour and the small pleasures of life. But the air was different tonight, charged with something unnameable. The shadows of the pony and cart flickered against the hedgerows, leading them ever closer to the gusset.

From the bushy hedgerow, the boy heard a soft, pathetic murmur. He commanded the pony to stop. The young lad—

James M'Ghee—walked toward the sound. There, against the wooden palings, he noticed a bundle under the moonlight. The pathetic murmur had ceased, and as he got closer, he could see exactly what it was—the bundle was that of a woman covered in blood, a nasty gash in her throat—silent now—nothing—just a body under the ghostly moonlight.

M'Ghee shouted, "Help! Someone help! Help!"

The miners, drawn by the frantic cry, quickened their pace, their chatter abruptly silenced by the urgency in the boy's voice. As they hurried closer, they noticed a figure standing along the edge of the road, partially obscured by shadow. The man was watching from a distance, still and silent, as if undecided whether to come forward or vanish into the night. His outline was barely visible, but the glint of white canvas shoes gave him away, contrasting with his dark clothing and the dim glow of the moon.

"what's happened?" one miner shouted, his voice slicing through the night air.

James pointed, trembling. "over here! A woman...... she's hurt!"

In the dim moonlight, the miners noticed the torn clothes clinging to her body, her bare legs streaked with blood—a deep, ragged gash across her neck, blood still slick and wet—her pale face ghostly. Someone raised a lantern, throwing a harsh glow over the scene. The miners shouted for help.

One of the miners pointed toward the figure at the hedgerow. "Who's that?" he muttered, his voice cutting through the still air.

Then, another miner caught sight of the figure and, almost instinctively, shouted, "Look! … it's that nigger.. that boxer!"

A murmur spread among the miners, shifting into an accusatory tone as more noticed him. "Negro," another voice whispered, harsh with suspicion. The whispers quickly became shouts, the men's words fuelled by fear and unease, gathering into a chorus of blame. The man standing at the hedgerow tensed, the hostility in their voices unmistakable.

Finally, with the miners' words echoing around him, he took a step back and then another. Their accusations grew louder, their voices harsh in the quiet night, and with one last glance at the crowd, the man turned and fled—disappearing swiftly down the hedgerow-lined Summerlee Road, slipping into the darkness toward the valley cradling the Mossend Iron and Steelworks. The miners followed in pursuit.

In no time, a crowd gathered, villagers drawn from their homes, their faces lit by lanterns and the moon's eerie glow. They moved toward the source of the commotion, a mix of curiosity and dread knitting together as they closed in on the scene.

"Stand back!" someone ordered. It was only a fleeting time before the police arrived. A doctor followed close behind, his expression grave as he knelt beside the woman. Silence swept over the onlookers.

A short distance away, a retired miner, Henry Welsh, opened the front door of his whitewashed cottage, drawn by the commotion. The whispers of villagers drifted toward him, curious and anxious, pulling him closer to the gathering crowd.

He shuffled through the throng, dread pooling in his stomach as he made his way to the front. And there, against the rotting wooden palings, lay the motionless body of his wife, Mary Jane. Known to every soul in town, she was now nothing more than a ghostly figure on the cold ground.

Low voices passed between the doctor and the police, their words swallowed by the tense quiet. A stretcher was brought, and men carried the woman's body away, her lifeless form swaying gently in time with their steps. As the crowd began to thin, whispers surfaced, drifting among the villagers like a dark undercurrent. "Dark skin," a miner muttered. "Negro," another voice whispered. "That boxer."

The words spread, faint at first but soon loud enough to fill the night air with a sharp, uneasy weight. They knew who had fled into the darkness. They had seen him at the fairground, watched him fight, his figure familiar in the ring. But here, in the narrow streets of Larkhall, he was no longer just a showman. Under the moonlit sky, Pasha had become something else entirely.

He was a shadow fleeing into the darkness, already guilty in the eyes of the town.

THE CHASE

The sharp thud of footsteps broke through the stillness of the cobbled streets. A desperate young man dashed through the narrow alleys, his thin frame darting from shadow to shadow, trying to escape something far worse than darkness. Each breath came in desperate gulps; his shirt clung to his back, damp with sweat.

The mob thundered forward. Lanterns bobbed and swayed, their light slicing across the walls. Each shout stirred sleepers from their beds, and the miners' hardened faces revealed no pity. These men—miners mostly, their faces hard as stone—no longer saw a person running. He was a quarry, a shadow to be hunted down before dawn broke.

"Get him!" one voice rose above the others, cracking like a whip through the frigid air. But the young man pressed on, weaving through the maze of narrow streets, a surge of panic pounding in his chest. Every corner brought a fresh surge of dread as the village seemed to close on him.

From windows, villagers watched the scene unfold, women muttering to each other in hushed voices, children peering through half-opened doors. Word of murder had swept through the streets, sparking the kind of fear that fuelled the crowd's chase, each rumour sharper than the last. The village, usually as still as the dead this time of night, had woken to the smell of blood.

The young man turned into an alley. For a heartbeat, he thought he had lost them, his back pressing into the cold stone, his body still with terror. But the sound of boots and swinging lanterns filled the air again, shadows creeping close, flickers of light catching on the corner of his shirt as he ducked into another passage.

Exhaustion began to gnaw at him, each step harder than the last, each breath a sharp slice through his lungs. He forced himself forward, searching for someplace to hide, somewhere the flickering lights could not reach.

He reached the outbuildings of the colliery. He darted across the lane without a second thought, slipping into one building and then an office. Pasha crouched low in the dimly lit office, pressing himself back into the corner, his heart pounding against his ribs. Dust filled the air, and the cool wood of the cabinet against his back offered only a slight sense of safety. But it was all too familiar—the feeling of being exposed, vulnerable—just like that day in Mafeking.

Then, it had been the cracked earth beneath him, the burning sand against his skin, and the lone anthill he had clung to as Mauser bullets ripped through the air. Each shot slammed into the anthill, the impact echoing through his bones as he pressed himself lower, hoping to disappear.

He was hiding again – this time in the shadowed corner of an office. And this time, it was not gunfire slicing through the night—it was the crowd's shouts, carrying his name like a weapon, filled with fury. Their voices hammered in his mind, louder and harsher than any bullet, filling him with dread just as cutting. Like the anthill before it, this office was no more than a thin shield. He knew it would not hold for long.

Morning arrived as a dull, unforgiving light, casting grey over the village's stone buildings. The mob was no longer the frenzied force it had been but had not given up. They moved with cold intent, voices low as they scoured every street and alley. They moved to the colliery buildings.

There, they found him. Huddled in the dark, knees drawn to his chest, he squinted against the lanterns' harsh light as they pulled him up. His bare feet, raw and bleeding, could take him no further.

When the sergeant finally arrested Liffey, no fight was left in him. He stood silent as the cold metal cuffs bit into his wrists. "They're too tight," he muttered, but the words felt distant even to himself, swallowed by the oppressive weight of what was to come.

He walked barefoot beside the officer in silence, his eyes flickering across the fields, but there was no escape now. His feet ached - somewhere along his escape, he had discarded the white canvas shoes in the fields. He barely remembered doing it, the night's panic blurring into a haze.

The Larkhall Police Station was small and suffocating, and by the time Liffey was locked inside, the town had already begun to stir with the news. It spread like wildfire. Whispers turned into loud murmurs, faces pressed against windows, and soon, the streets were alive with angry voices. He could hear them outside, a growing mass of people shouting, their fury spilling into the narrow roads. They wanted him to hang. Not tomorrow. Now.

The plan was simple: the police would get him on the train to Hamilton by eleven. But nothing in this town would ever be simple again. When word leaked out, the crowd surged. Men and women lined the road from the prison to the station. Their eyes were wild, some with fear, some with the thrill of bloodlust, and others with that strange curiosity that always follows tragedy.

By the time the train arrived, the mob had grown thick, filling the air with venomous chants. Police lined the path, but Liffey could feel the heat of their rage pressing against him. They hurled insults—some threw stones.

"Hang him!" came the cry from somewhere in the throng.

A miner's fist swung out, missing him by inches, and Liffey shrank closer to the officers at his side. His legs trembled beneath him. He saw the faces blurred together, twisted in hatred and disbelief, as if they could not quite fathom the man before them, a showman and a boxer —this broken figure with a "Basuto face" they so quickly blamed.

The officers moved him through the sea of bodies, each measured and hurried step. Another stone flew past his head. Liffey could barely breathe. He wanted to disappear into the earth, stop time, and undo whatever had led him to this moment. He glanced back once—just once—and caught sight of a woman in the crowd, her face streaked with tears. Maybe she knew Mrs. Welsh. Maybe she mourned for her. Or she mourned for them all.

He was shoved onto the train, and as the doors slammed shut, the chorus of hisses from the crowd grew louder, followed by the hiss of the steam engine beginning to move. He was leaving Larkhall behind, but its weight pressed on his chest like a stone he could never throw off.

Hamilton was quieter, but it offered no peace. He was ushered through the streets and into the cold walls of the County Buildings. Sheriff Thomson barely looked at him as the charges were read. Rape. Murder. The words echoed in the hollow chamber of his mind.

"I didn't..." he began to whisper, but no one was listening.

That night, alone in Duke Street Jail, he stared at the stone ceiling, hearing the distant water drip from some hidden pipe. His thoughts drifted to home, to Lesotho, where the mountains had felt like protection. Now, they felt like another lifetime.

Liffey's hand trembled in the darkness as he touched his face, which they all recognised. The face that had damned him before the trial had even begun.

THE TRIAL

It was October 24, 1905. Outside the Circuit Court of Judiciary in Glasgow, the cold of early autumn had settled like an invisible presence, chilling the air.

"My name is Pasha Liffey, a native of Mafeteng, Basutoland. I am unmarried, 24 years of age, a groom, and have no fixed residence. I prefer not to say anything regarding the charge of Rape and Murder preferred against me."

Pasha's voice was steady but hollow as the words drifted into the silence of the courtroom.

He stood in the dock, a small but stocky figure dwarfed by the vast expanse of the room. Towering stone walls loomed and hugged the silence.

The high ceiling stretched far above, trapping the weight of judgment that seemed to press down on everyone present.

Witnesses, spectators, jurors, and officials fixed their eyes on the young man in the dock. Pasha's slight frame stood out starkly in the courtroom, his dark eyes steady but distant, as if he were already somewhere far away, beyond the reach of the cold justice about to be dispensed.

From the press box, an illustrator sat quietly. Her charcoal sticks moved effortlessly - even passionately, her strokes quick, sharp, and blunt on the rough cartridge paper - capturing the likeness of a man whose slight, small frame seemed lost in the room's vastness.

Charles Scott Dickson, His Majesty's Advocate, rose slowly from his seat, his eyes narrowing as they locked on the figure in the dock. The scrape of his chair echoed through the courtroom like a prelude to something final.

His voice, when it came, was cold and precise.

"On August 11, 1905, you, Pasha Liffey, did ravish and murder Mary Jane Welsh."

The accusation landed heavily. The spectators leaned forward, their eyes fixed on the prosecutor, their ears straining to catch every word.

In the streets of Glasgow, news of the crime had spread like wildfire, a brutal tale of a woman found dead of night, her throat slashed, her body abandoned on the cold stones of Dykehead Road. And now this man, this stranger, stood accused.

Dickson's voice was sharp, slicing through the room with each word. "You beat her. You stabbed her. You cut her throat and left her to die."

Pasha did not flinch. His dark eyes remained focused on some distant point, his expression unreadable. But the words reverberated through the room, heavy with the weight of finality.

The illustrator's hand continued to move across the page, capturing the stillness in Pasha's posture and the strange calm in his face.

The widower, Henry Welsh, was called. His face, pale and etched with grief, seemed to sag as he approached the stand. His hands trembled as he spoke, his voice thin and broken. "I found her… lying there on the road … there was blood everywhere."

With his trademark Homburg hat, the journalist, who had been capturing the moments, glanced briefly at the illustrator, who was capturing the widower's grief.

Sergeant Stewart's testimony followed, cold and clinical. "Her throat was cut deep," his tone detached. "There was much blood." He added, "We found a knife at the scene, covered in blood. And a jacket, later identified as belonging to the accused."

The courtroom's collective gaze shifted toward Pasha once again as if the weight of the evidence had already rendered its judgment. Yet, Pasha stood there, unmoving, his slight figure cast in the long shadows of the towering walls.

The witnesses came and went. John McLuckie spoke of the blood on the road the morning after the murder. James Carberry, just a boy, described seeing Pasha lying in the street that night, thinking him drunk, unaware of the horror that had taken place just beyond his sight.

The tension in the circuit courtroom built with each testimony.

Then came the final blow. William Adamson, the boxing circus owner who had employed Pasha for years, took the stand. His words were sombre. "That knife…… it belonged to Pasha. I've seen it many times."

He hesitated before adding, "And the jacket—they found it near the body—it's his too."

Adamson's words cut deep, leaving no room for doubt. "He was a good man when sober," Adamson continued, his voice faltering slightly. "But when he drank..." The rest of the sentence went unsaid, but it was clear enough.

The room felt colder, the air heavier, as if even the walls sensed what was about to come.

The jury returned quickly, their decision already written on their faces. The foreman stood, his voice cutting through the thick silence of the courtroom.

"Guilty."

Every human in the court stirred, shifting uneasily in their seats, releasing a collective breath they had not realised they were holding. The judge's voice was firm, almost emotionless, as he pronounced the sentence: "Death by hanging!"

The silence that followed was more profound than any that had come before. It was the silence of finality, of death, of fate. Pasha Liffey, the man who had once dodged bullets and delivered messages of hope, was now condemned by something far more insidious—something inevitable.

Pasha was led from the courtroom, his footsteps heavy on the cold stone floor. His head remained high, his face expressionless, as though he had already accepted what was to come. Outside, the city of Glasgow continued, indifferent to the fate of the man they had sentenced to die. The world, as it always did, moved on.

But inside the courtroom, the silence lingered. The creak of the benches and the shuffle of feet faded into the grim stillness.

The journalist watched Pasha disappear, the memory of Mafeking flickering briefly in his mind. The man from Mafeteng—the runner, the fighter, the wanderer—was swallowed by the shadows, and all that was left was the silence.

The illustrator laid down her charcoal stick. Indelibly captured, Pasha's soul was on the cartridge paper.

A FINAL VISIT

He stood tall, his dark wool suit pristine, every line of fabric pressed into quiet authority. Even here, in the stark confines of Duke Street Prison, not a speck of dust clung to him. His tie, a neat bow, was set with precise care. The reverend took great pride in his appearance—not out of vanity, but discipline, a reflection of his unwavering respect for the weight of this occasion.

His spectacles caught the flickering light as he surveyed the room, his gaze calm and deliberate. The thin wire frames were practical, like everything about him—measured, controlled.

The prison clerk glanced up, his eyes flicking over the reverend's immaculate presence before returning to the task at hand. He opened the thick register, the worn pages whispering against the counter. Pen poised, he hesitated—just slightly. The reverend had seen it before. The unfamiliar name, the moment of uncertainty. With a quiet nod, he stepped forward and took the pen from the clerk's outstretched hand, the gesture smooth, assured.

He printed his name—**Reverend Édouard Jacottet**—each letter deliberate, the penmanship of a man who valued precision in both word and action. Then, with the same measured care, he signed it.

The clerk leaned forward, eyes narrowing at the foreign script. The pause stretched between them, filled with something unsaid.

Jacottet let it settle, unbothered. He had long learned the weight of silence.

The register slid back across the counter. The entry was complete.

A warden, standing nearby with an impassive expression, glanced at the page. He, too, took a moment to register the name. But no questions followed. None were necessary. The reverend's presence—the crisp lines of his suit, the quiet gravity behind his spectacles—spoke for itself.

Beyond them, the iron door loomed. Thick, unyielding. A barrier between the reverend and the prisoner. The warden stepped forward, key in hand, and began the slow, deliberate process of unlocking it.

Jacottet remained still, shoes planted firmly on the cold stone floor. Polished, but not showy. A reflection of his quiet dignity. His fingers rested lightly on the counter as the lock gave a heavy, grinding click.

The door groaned open, its sound reverberating down the corridor.

Jacottet straightened, his hands folding together. His perfectly draped coat rustled faintly as he moved forward. The weight of the visit—the gravity of what lay ahead—pressed in around him, but his composure remained unshaken.

The name he had written in the register would remain, a record of his presence in this cold, grey place. Soon, he would stand before Pasha Liffey. His role in this final chapter was about to begin.

The iron door groaned shut behind him.

The reverend stopped briefly, allowing his eyes to adjust to the dim light.

A faint flicker from the hearth cast wavering shadows on the rough stone walls, the only warmth in a room otherwise frozen in time.

Pasha sat by the fire.

The weak glow barely reached the far corners of the cell. His face, half in shadow, was lined with fatigue, older than his years.

Jacottet's gaze settled on him.

The boy he had once known—the lively, restless spirit that had run through the plains of Basutoland—was nearly unrecognizable. Yet, as their eyes met, something flickered. A moment of understanding.

The reverend moved forward, his footsteps soft against the stone. The chair creaked as Pasha shifted slightly, but his eyes remained fixed on the fire.

The silence between them was heavy.

Finally, Jacottet spoke, his voice low and steady, barely louder than the crackling hearth.

"Pasha."

Pasha turned his head slowly, his eyes meeting Jacottet's, dark hollows beneath them.

His lips parted, but no words came at first. When he finally spoke, his voice was rough, as though unused for hours.

"I knew you'd come."

Jacottet pulled a chair from the side of the room and sat beside him. The reverend's presence was still and solid, like a rock against the tide. He took in the dim surroundings—the iron bars, the cold stone, the hearth struggling to keep the dark at bay—and knew that no words he offered could alter what was to come. Still, he had not come to provide easy comfort but something deeper, more challenging to grasp in such moments.

Pasha shifted in his chair, his gaze returning to the fire. "I've been sitting here thinking," he murmured, his voice quieter now, as if speaking more to himself than the reverend. "About the end... about what comes next. I'm unsure what frightens me more—the thought of nothing or what I might find."

Jacottet leaned forward, his elbows resting on his knees. "There's peace for you, Pasha, if you let it in."

Pasha's eyes closed, his fingers gripping the arms of the chair. "They say I've done terrible things. You know that. Things that can't be undone."

The reverend nodded, his face solemn. "We all carry our burdens, Pasha. But the road doesn't end here. What matters now is what's in your heart in these final hours."

The fire cast fleeting shadows across the walls. Jacottet reached into his coat and pulled out the small, worn Bible that had travelled with him from Basutoland. He opened it slowly, his fingers tracing the familiar pages as if drawing strength from the words. The verses he chose were in Sesotho, the language of their shared past, of the mission station where Pasha had once been a boy, where the world seemed full of endless possibilities.

As the reverend read, his voice soft and deep, the words rolled over the room like a dark tide, carrying them both back to the past. "Jehova ke modisa wa ka..." The verses spoke of the Lord as a shepherd, of finding rest even in the shadow of death. Each word felt heavier in the silence, a reminder that even now, in this darkest of moments, there was a flicker of something beyond the cold stone and iron bars.

Pasha closed his eyes, the tension easing from his shoulders, his body sinking deeper into the chair. The fire glowed faintly, its warmth spreading weakly into the room, though it felt more like a memory of warmth than the real thing.

When the reading was over, Jacottet closed the Bible carefully, placing it on his lap as he watched Pasha, whose eyes remained closed.

"It's been so long since I heard those words," Pasha murmured, his voice softer now, almost fragile. "In my language, it feels like home again."

Jacottet nodded, understanding the weight of what those words meant for a man so far from home. He could see the battle inside

Pasha—fear and guilt wrestling against the flicker of peace he was trying to hold on to.

Without a word, Jacottet stood and moved to the floor, kneeling beside the hearth. He gestured for Pasha to join him. Slowly, Pasha rose from the chair, his body stiff and heavy with exhaustion, and knelt beside him. The reverend took his hands, their fingers intertwined in the dim light, and they bowed their heads together.

The following prayer was spoken in Sesotho, a soft murmur in the dark. Jacottet's voice was steady, but his words were solemn. This gravity matched the flickering firelight around them. He prayed for peace, for Pasha's soul to find rest. He prayed for forgiveness, not just from God, but from the man kneeling beside him. He prayed for strength in the hours ahead, knowing that Pasha's journey was not yet done. The words rose slowly, like smoke from the hearth, filling the air between them.

As they knelt together, Pasha's breathing slowed, his hands loosening slightly in Jacottet's grasp. There was no grand moment of revelation, no sudden release of all the pain and fear that had weighed on him for so long. But there was peace, small and quiet, settling like ash in the cold air.

When the prayer was finished, they sat in silence, the fire flickering, and the only movement in the room was the fire. When Pasha opened his eyes, they held a quiet acceptance, though the shadows remained.

"I'm ready."

Jacottet looked at him, his heart heavy with the weight of that simple statement. He nodded once, standing slowly, helping Pasha to his feet. They stood together, the silence between them profound and thick. No more words were needed. The reverend placed a hand on Pasha's shoulder, a final gesture, before stepping back toward the iron door.

As it opened, the lock turning echoed down the corridor. Jacottet paused, looking back at the man standing by the hearth, his shadow long and dark against the wall. In the last glow of the coals, they both knew—this was the last time they would meet.

Jacottet stepped through the door without another word, leaving behind the fading warmth of the hearth and the man who had once been a boy, far from home.

SILENT REFLECTIONS

The silence after the reverend left was thick, pressing down on Pasha like a weight. Barefoot, he stood on the smooth cobblestones, feeling the familiar bite of cold beneath his feet. Ten days—that was how long he had been here. Yet already, it felt like the walls were all he had ever known.

He knelt at the hearth, his hands moving with quiet purpose, stacking kindling and coaxing a flame with a careful breath. The soft crackle of fire broke the stillness, licking the logs with quiet hunger. He stepped back, feeling the warmth press against his skin, chasing away the damp chill that clung to the cell.

Pasha pulled the chair closer, its legs scraping roughly over the floor. He sat, the flickering light casting long shadows against the walls. He lit his pipe, inhaling deeply, the taste of tobacco filling his lungs. Smoke curled upward, and for a moment, the hard edges of the cell softened.

He let his mind drift.......

.........*Glasgow. The laughter of crowds. The thrill of the stage. Four years ago, he had stood just yards from here, performing in the Savage South Africa show. The night Queen Victoria died, the spectacle had paused—briefly. The audience had stood in solemn silence, heads bowed for the empire's great matriarch, then resumed their seats as if nothing had changed.*

But things had changed.

Even further back, he saw himself at Earl's Court, lifting his voice in tribute to the Queen's 80th birthday. That day, the empire had felt untouchable—its reach vast, its grip unbreakable. He had been part of its spectacle, paraded as the warrior of its lands. The crowds had cheered, and he had let himself believe, for a moment, that their admiration was real.

But cheers never lasted. The crowd always moved on.

The fire flickered, casting restless light against the stone. He thought of Basutoland—the plains, the heat, the wind. He had run free once, his strength effortless, his breath easy. Now, even his memories of home felt distant, like echoes of a life that no longer belonged to him.

The streets of Glasgow came next. The sharp air, the cobbles slick with rain, the crowds shifting past him, blind to his presence. He had fought for something he couldn't name, chasing dreams that dissolved like smoke. He had dazzled, performed, survived. But it had always been a performance. And in the end, the world had written him out of its story.

The fire burned, but even it would die soon.

Reverend Jacottet's visit lingered in his mind. The reverend had spoken in Sesotho—their language, their homeland woven into every syllable. Those words had carried something more than faith. A warmth no fire could match. He had talked of peace, of redemption, but Pasha knew better. The world had already decided. No prayer could change that.

And yet, even as hope faded, he was grateful. The reverend had spoken to him as a man, not as a condemned soul. They had prayed together, their voices rising into the still air, dissolving like the smoke from the fire.

The flames crackled softly. Their glow dimmed. The cold crept back in.

One of the wardens, McDonald, lingered by the door, his presence quiet but intent. Unlike the others, he had listened. He had spoken with Pasha, shared stories, and filled the daily log with more than just routine notes. His entries were not just records of a prisoner's final days but glimpses into the man behind the sentence—alive, reflective, human.

Now, as he studied Pasha's face, it was as if he were searching for something—understanding, perhaps, or simply the weight of what could never be written down. He had written more, observed more, and captured what others ignored. But words could only go so far.

The fire would burn out eventually. There was peace in that.

Pasha glanced at the Bible beside him. It had been a comfort these past days—not for salvation, but for understanding. The weight of it in his hands grounded him. But even those words felt distant now.

The fire had all but died, its embers faint and spent. He could feel it—the slowing of his breath, the heaviness in his limbs. He wasn't afraid. He had seen the fire burn bright, felt its heat, and now, as it cooled, so did he.

The silence returned, thick and heavy, wrapping around him. His pipe lay cold in his hand. His eyes drifted shut. The rise and fall of his chest grew slower. Outside, the world continued, but here, it no longer mattered.

The fire had burned its course.

As the last ember faded to ash, so did the world around him. The cold deepened, the silence pressed close, and at that moment, Pasha—now only prisoner 14723—felt the call again.

The distant caw of the crow.

Wrapping him in its wings.

Guiding him into the night.

But just as he began to drift away, a sharp rattle at the cell doors cut through the silence.

A voice.

"Pasha, come with me."

THROUGH THE BLACK DRAPES

The chamber felt like a tomb. Heavy black drapes lined the walls, absorbing the dim glow from the overhead light. The air was thick, oppressive, and stagnant. The room's chill seeped into the skin, gnawing at any trace of warmth.

He stood there, still as death, broad-shouldered in his white shirt and braces—the executioner. The stiff collar bit into his neck as his breath came slow and steady, each puff of his pipe smoke curling lazily into the air before being swallowed by the darkness. He wasn't in any hurry. Time did not belong to the condemned, nor to him. It was merely a formality.

In the centre of the room's wooden floor was a trapdoor—its edges barely visible beneath the muted light. A single chalk line was drawn across it, thin and pale, like a scar etched in anticipation. Every detail of this grim rehearsal mattered. Soon, another man would stand there, waiting.

The door creaked open, and there he was—Pasha, barefoot. He hesitated, his eyes adjusting to the dim light, taking in the scene before him: the trapdoor, the black drapes on the walls, the faint scent of pipe smoke and whisky in the air.

The man in braces and rolled sleeves said nothing, his eyes fixed on Pasha with the calm indifference of someone who had seen the end too many times. He puffed on his pipe, the smoke drifting lazily upwards.

Pasha entered the room cautiously, his feet making soft sounds against the cold stone. He could feel the weight of the man's gaze on him, how his eyes followed every movement, calculating and detached—the quiet authority of someone who knew exactly what was coming loomed like a second shadow.

"Take off your clothes. Stand up straight," the man ordered, his voice thick and slurred, each word a measured drop in the heavy air. Pasha complied, his back straightening under the command. The man stepped forward, hands rough and heavy as they gripped Pasha's shoulders, measuring his height with a practised hand. The touch was clinical, devoid of humanity, like a craftsman handling a piece of wood before cutting.

He pulled out a small notebook, the pages worn and creased from years of use, and scribbled something down. His eyes flicked up to Pasha's face briefly before returning to his task, his expression one of detached professionalism.

"Let's see what we're working with," he muttered, more to himself than to Pasha. He shoved him toward the corner of the chamber where there was a scale. "Step on," he ordered flatly, as though this was just another step in a mechanical ritual.

Pasha stepped onto the scale, the cold metal pressing against his feet. The man leaned in, scanning the numbers before scribbling them down. "Hmm—one hundred and thirty-five pounds. Heavy for your kind at five foot three," he mused, his lips curling into a faint, mirthless smile. "You have a very thick neck."

Something was behind those words—a faint note of condescension, something dark and unspoken. He paused, tapping the pencil against his teeth, his gaze lingering on Pasha's bare shoulders. Then he leaned in, close enough that Pasha could smell the whisky on his breath, sharp and sour.

"You are my fortieth—and my first darkie in Scotland," his voice low, almost amused. "Lucky you. Me? I am Henry Pierrepoint. But call me Harry."

Pasha's expression remained unreadable, though a slight stiffening of his jaw betrayed his discomfort. His eyes darted toward the chalk line on the floor, drawn across the trapdoor. Pierrepoint didn't shove him—he didn't need to. His presence alone did the pushing, pulling Pasha toward that line with every breath.

"Stand on the line," Pierrepoint grunted, his voice thick with authority. His hand gripped Pasha's arm, guiding him toward the trapdoor with a roughness that left no room for hesitation. "Let's see how you fit."

Pasha stepped onto the line, his bare feet hovering over the trapdoor. The cold of the wood seeped into him, grounding him in the moment's reality. He did not need to look down to know where he stood. He could feel it in his bones.

Pierrepoint stepped forward, closing the gap between them. His breath, heavy with whisky and tobacco, lingered like a physical presence in the space between them.

The man tapped Pasha lightly on the head, a condescending gesture with no meaning other than the need to assert control. Then, with a cruel smile curling at the corners of his mouth, he ordered, "Now, on your knees."

The order was like a blow. There was no hesitation, no room for protest. Pasha's legs buckled beneath him, his knees hitting the cold floor with a dull thud. Pierrepoint watched him with detached satisfaction as though this was another predictable step in a grim dance.

Pierrepoint stood over him, his pipe hanging loosely from his mouth. His hand reached out again, resting heavily on Pasha's head. He gave another light tap as if testing the weight of him, the way a butcher might test meat on a slab.

"There you go, darkie," Pierrepoint murmured, his voice mockingly soft, dripping with false gentleness. "Now you're free to go."

The words clung to the air, thick with cruel irony, settling over the chamber like the black drapes on the walls. Pierrepoint stepped back, leaving Pasha kneeling alone on the cold stone floor, the weight of the moment pressing down on them both.

For Pasha, the silence in the room was heavier than Pierrepoint's presence. He stayed on his knees, his bare skin against the unforgiving floor, the chalk line beneath him a barrier he could not cross. The man in braces turned, his steps echoing as he left the room. The door shut behind him, leaving Pasha alone in the suffocating stillness.

The air seemed to grow colder, the light dimmer, as though the room was shrinking. Pasha inhaled deeply, his breaths slow and deliberate, the faint scent of smoke lingering in his nostrils. He closed his eyes, his mind drifting backwards to the sunlit plains of Basutoland, the warmth of home, the fleeting freedom he had once known.

As the faint sound of Pierrepoint's footsteps faded down the corridor, the chamber became silent again. Pasha remained kneeling, the cold of the floor a steady reminder of the inevitability that loomed just beyond the heavy drapes.

THE COLD STORAGE OF JUSTICE

November 16, 1905

D awn crept over Glasgow in shades of iron and pale light, pressing down against the city's chimneyed rooftops and stone-cobbled streets. It was a grey morning, unremarkable yet thick with the quiet stirrings of something final. The city moved as it always did—markets opening, trams rattling, factory whistles cutting through the cold air—but elsewhere, in the quiet halls of its institutions, Pasha Liffey was being tidied away.

At Barlinnie Prison, a clerk sat at a polished wooden desk, his ink-stained fingers poised over the register. The great book was thick, its pages worn at the edges, heavy with names that no longer mattered. He worked methodically, as he always did, recording the necessary details with an efficiency that left no room for sentiment.

Name of prisoner: Pasha Liffey
Date of execution: November 15, 1905
Time of death: 8:00 a.m.
Cause of death: Judicial hanging

The pen scraped against the parchment, each stroke of ink pressing Pasha deeper into the annals of official history. The register was closed, the name locked in.

Elsewhere in the prison, another book lay open—the daily log, where each shift's warden noted the prisoner's final days. Here, McDonald had written more than most. His entries were not

196

simply routine: they were observations, reflections, small moments captured between a warden and a condemned man.

"He asked if the sunrise was visible. I told him no, but the sky was brightening. He nodded, said nothing more."

"A quiet man. Does not weep. Seems to think a lot before he speaks."

McDonald's hand had lingered on the page before reading the final line:

"At peace. No trouble."

When the last of the prison documents were gathered, they were sealed inside an official envelope, stamped with the warden's signature, and sent south.

As the prison turned its focus back to the living, elsewhere in the city, other records were being assembled.

At the High Court of Justiciary, clerks moved through oak-panelled rooms, retrieving court transcripts, trial notes, and depositions. The witness statements—some carefully written, others scrawled hastily—were gathered together, each a fragment of the story that had led Pasha to the noose. There was the judge's final ruling, the appeal that never stood a chance, the letter from the governor confirming there would be no reprieve.

All of it was bundled, wrapped in twine, and marked for transfer.

By afternoon, these papers had joined those from the prison, locked inside a leather satchel for their journey to Edinburgh. The wheels of the mail coach clattered over the cobbled streets, carrying Pasha's life away in the form of ink, paper, and signatures.

The General Register House sat like a fortress on Princes Street, its high stone walls guarding the history of Scotland. Inside, under the glow of gas lamps, clerks worked in quiet efficiency, their desks lined with stacks of documents waiting to be processed.

William MacNair was among them, a young man with an eye for order and a mind that rarely strayed from his work. He received the latest delivery without ceremony, lifting the heavy satchel onto his desk and unfastening the leather straps.

Inside, the papers were as expected: death certificates, trial records, execution reports. He read each one as he stacked them, aligning the pages with the precision of a man who understood the importance of small details.

The final pages were those from Barlinnie. The register entry. The warden's log. McDonald's words caught his attention, their tone different from the usual cold efficiency of prison records. He read them twice before placing them with the others.

MacNair took a length of ribbon, threading it carefully through the pages, securing them into a single bound volume. A pool of crimson wax melted onto the ribbon's knot, hardening as he pressed the official seal into it. The story was now set.

He carried the volume to the archive chambers, where the deep drawers of the iron cabinets waited. Here, names were not spoken, only recorded, locked away in numbered compartments to be forgotten by all but history itself.

MacNair slid the volume into its place. The cabinet door closed with a quiet, final thud.

Outside, the evening had settled, the last light of day turning the city to a dull shade of silver. Footsteps echoed down the marble halls of the General Register House as the clerks finished their work. Doors locked. Lamps dimmed.

Pasha Liffey had been a man of flesh and blood. He had walked the streets of Glasgow, told stories, felt the sun on his skin. Now, he was a file in an archive. A name pressed into ink. A case closed.

In the city, a tram rattled past, its passengers caught in the quiet worries of everyday life. The news of the morning's execution was already fading into distant conversation.

Inside the vault, Pasha's story rested under the careful guard of ink, iron, and time.

And there it would remain, unseen and untouched, until history decided to take another look.

THE EDITOR'S DESK

Cape Town, November 1905.

The news of Pasha's execution reached the editor's desk with a soft rustle as the clerk slid an envelope across the wooden surface. Peregrino unfolded the telegram with care, each movement slow and steady as though bracing himself for its weight.

The words were simple and stark:

"Pasha Liffey executed at Duke Street Prison, Glasgow, November 15, 1905."

He reread it, each word sinking deeper, hammering against his sense of justice.

He had expected it, of course. There had been little hope for mercy—not for a man like Pasha Liffey. In a foreign land, far from home, accused of a vile crime, Liffey's fate had been sealed long before the trial ended. But the finality of it—the cold, clinical language of the telegram—stirred something heavy in Peregrino's chest.

He set the telegram down gently as though it might shatter under the weight of its meaning. Rising from his desk, he moved to the window and gazed out at the restless streets of Cape Town. The sounds of the city—street vendors calling, children laughing, the clatter of hooves on cobblestones—felt distant and muted. Beyond the noise and bustle, he saw the sea stretching into the horizon. Somewhere beyond that vast expanse of water, a man had died, condemned and forgotten.

This case had begun months ago. Rumours of a Basuto man in Scotland, accused of the brutal murder of an old woman in Larkhall. The details had trickled in like a foul tide, staining the papers with their lurid headlines. Pasha Liffey—an African, a foreigner, a man without means or friends to defend him—had been all but convicted in the court of public opinion long before the judge pronounced the sentence.

And now it was done. The rope had snapped, the body had fallen, and the world would go on as if nothing had changed. But Peregrino knew better. This was not just the death of one man. This was the beginning of something darker, something that would cling to the skin of every Black man and woman in Britain and beyond.

His hand rested against the windowpane, the cool glass grounding him in the moment. His thoughts returned to Liffey and the bitter truths he'd come to know so well: justice was seldom the same for Black men as it was for whites. It was a different kind of justice, heavy with prejudice and steeped in fear.

A knock at the door broke his reverie. His assistant, a quiet young man with sharp eyes and ink-stained fingers, stepped inside.

"More news from Glasgow," the assistant said, holding a neatly folded newspaper. "It's more details about Liffey."

Peregrino took it, nodding his thanks. He unfolded the page slowly, feeling the weight of the words before reading them. The article was what he expected—stark, clinical, devoid of sympathy. Pasha Liffey was reduced to a figure, a statistic, a warning.

The editor's jaw clenched. He felt the familiar stir of anger beneath his calm exterior. It would be easy to lash out, fill his paper with venom, and let the ink spill his outrage. But that wasn't his way. His voice had to be measured and reasoned. He had seen too many men lose themselves in a fury; their words turned into weapons against their cause.

No, he would not allow them that satisfaction. He had to be better, and his readers needed him to be better.

He returned to his desk, the clipping still in hand, and sat heavily in his chair. His fingers brushed the edge of the telegram, the moment's weight settling in his bones. This would be a more complex editorial—a plea, a warning, a reckoning.

He reached for his typewriter, the familiar weight of it grounding him. His hands hovered over the keys, motionless. What could he say that would matter? What words could cut through the fog of prejudice, fear, and hate?

He glanced at the clipping again, rereading the language used to describe Pasha. The words, stark and detached, painted a picture of a monster, not a man.

Peregrino took a deep breath and began to type.

"The news of the execution of Pasha Liffey, the Basuto, has sent a thrill of horror through the whole civilised community of coloured people. It is my fervent hope that this bloodthirsty and horrible deed will not tend to create in the public mind a feeling of resentment and prejudice against the race as a whole."

His fingers moved steadily now, the words flowing as they always did when the subject was close to his heart. He had to remind them—and the world—that one man's guilt did not belong to an entire people. It was a simple truth but easily forgotten in times like these.

His thoughts wandered back to his time in Scotland, to Lanarkshire, where he had lived among people who had treated him with generosity and respect. They were not all like this, he reminded himself. But Pasha's death would change things. The fear, the suspicion—it would grow and spread.

He typed on.

"Let it not be said that we have forfeited the trust extended to us, for we come among you as students, as men of the professions, and we have ever treated your hospitality with respect. The actions of one must not stain the reputations of all."

The rhythm of the typewriter filled the room, a steady cadence that matched the urgency in his chest. He thought of the men and women who would read his words, those who looked to him for guidance, for clarity.

He typed his final lines with purpose:

"In the best interests of civilisation, of our common humanity, and for the protection of the unsophisticated as much as the refined, I pray that measures may be found to prevent the perpetuation of such dangers. Let us not allow this tragedy to add unwelcome chapters to the annals of criminality."

When he finished, the page was heavy with ink and conviction. He pulled it from the typewriter and read it over slowly, carefully. Every word had to count.

Satisfied, he handed the page to his assistant.

"Get this to the press soonest. The people must read this."

Peregrino leaned back in his chair as the assistant left, staring at the sunlight streaming through the window. The words were written, but the fight was far from over. The world was changing, and he had to believe his words could help steer it in the right direction—for Pasha, himself, and all of them.

FADING INTO EARTH

The year was 1958, and Glasgow stood on the brink of transformation. Sputnik had soared into the cosmos, Elvis crooned over wireless sets, and the nation's eyes turned eagerly toward the future. Yet, on Duke Street, the past still lingered. For centuries, Duke Street Prison had cast its shadow across the city's history, a hulking monument to punishment and power. Now, even its mighty walls could not withstand the tide of progress.

Demolition crews arrived at dawn, their heavy machinery rumbling like distant thunder. Bulldozers poised themselves against the weathered stone, ready to erase the site where countless lives had been locked away and forgotten. The northwest wall crumbled first, its thick masonry collapsing into heaps of rubble, a graveyard of memories buried in dust. The workers pressed steadily toward the southeast section, where the prison's darkest legacy lay.

Between 1902 and 1928, twelve souls had been hanged within those gaol's confines. Their bodies were interred in the prison yard, each grave marked by a simple headstone bearing only initials and dates. Unassuming markers for lives condemned and stories silenced. Among them lay Pasha Liffey, Scotland's first and only Black man to be executed. Like the others, his headstone stood quietly for decades, a weathered witness to time's relentless march.

As the bulldozers edged closer to the burial ground, the mood among the labourers shifted. The noisy banter of the morning faded into a solemn silence as they unearthed the graves. Headstones emerged from the weeds and overgrowth, their stark simplicity a reminder of the lives they represented. For a moment, the machines halted. The men stepped back, their usual chatter replaced by quiet reverence.

"Careful now," the foreman instructed - his voice subdued. "Handle them gently."

The labourers obeyed, lifting the stones by hand, their rough fingers brushing away decades of dirt and moss. These were not nameless graves; each marker bore the weight of a sentence, a story, a soul. Even the hardened foreman seemed to feel it, instructing his team to proceed with care. Among the stones, Pasha's initials caught the light for the last time before being catalogued and carried away.

By the early 1960s, the Ladywell housing scheme had risen on the site, its clean, modern flats a vision of progress. The bright windows and straight-edged facades stood as symbols of a new era, erasing the shadows of Duke Street's penal past. Yet, amid the development, a small patch of green remained—a quiet anomaly in the grid of urban renewal.

Some said the patch was left untouched out of respect for the dead, a silent acknowledgement of the ground's history. Others whispered of superstition, an unspoken reluctance to build over graves, even those long emptied. Whatever the reason, the patch of grass endured, its presence a subtle defiance against the forces that sought to bury the past.

For the families who moved into the Ladywell flats, the story of Duke Street Prison faded into whispers and folklore. Few knew the names of the twelve who had been executed, and fewer still had heard of Pasha Liffey. The headstones, once so carefully removed, vanished into the tides of time. Only the earth beneath the grass remembered, holding its secrets in the roots tangled deep in the soil.

In the years to come, children would play on that patch of green, oblivious to the lives beneath their feet. The laughter of youth replaced the silence of the forgotten. But for those who paused, stood still and felt the pull of history, the patch of grass carried a weight that could not be ignored.

The earth does not forget. The grass grew tall over what was lost, whispering to those who dared to listen. And though the headstones were gone, the memory of Pasha Liffey and the others lingered, quiet and persistent, a reminder that history's shadows can never truly be erased.

FOLLOW UP

November 2005

E wan Ravenscroft II stared at the leather suitcase sitting on the worn oak desk in his study. The initials "ER" embossed in gold caught the fading afternoon light, gleaming faintly, as if whispering secrets from another time. His fingers lingered on the brass latches, hesitant yet drawn to the stories that lay locked within. It had belonged to his grandfather, a man whose voice and convictions had shaped his family's legacy as journalists.

"This belonged to your grandfather. He reported on the Boer War and injustices few dared to touch. He believed stories had the power to change the world. You may find something in there worth carrying forward." Ewan's fingers traced the edges of an old typewriter, pens, and a cigarette holder nestled inside. But one thick envelope, slightly yellowed and frayed at the edges, caught his attention. It was marked: "Pasha" scribbled on the top left corner, "Follow Up."

He carefully opened the envelope, revealing a stack of hand-written notes from 1905. The words flowed in his grandfather's precise hand, still bold despite the passing of time. The notes detailed the trial of a man named Pasha, the first Black man to be executed in Scotland on November 15, 1905. His grandfather had been there, covering the case as part of his work on social injustices, following Pasha's life and the tragedy that had befallen him.

The further Ewan read the more profound the questions became. His grandfather had suspicions about the trial—witness testimonies were too similar, and the police's evidence was oddly convenient. Had Pasha been framed? The notes hinted at a manipulated narrative, a courtroom where the truth seemed more like a contrived performance than justice. There were suggestions of Pasha having an alias—Harry Henderson, and a curious note about a policeman identifying him by an old photograph linked to a past charge in Nottingham.

The phrase "Follow up" gnawed at Ewan, suggesting that his grandfather had intended to pursue the matter further, but something had stopped him. The suitcase, packed for decades, held a mystery frozen in time. Ewan felt the pull, the urge to pick up where his grandfather had left off.

UNEARTHING TRAGEDY

Ewan Ravenscroft stepped into the National Records of Scotland entrance hall, history echoing around him.

A faint scent hung in the air—a blend of aged paper with a vanilla-like sweetness, hints of dust and wood from old shelves. Beneath it all was a cool, mineral undertone, like the scent of clean stone, lending a grounding, almost mysterious quality to the space. He took in the silent, solemn atmosphere and approached the front desk, where a middle-aged clerk, neat-haired and with a no-nonsense expression, looked up from her logbook.

"Hello, I'm Ewan Ravenscroft. I have a booking to review records," glancing at his notebook. "AD15/05/112... it is about Pasha Liffey."

The clerk adjusted her glasses and nodded, briskly flipping through her entries. "Yes, Mr. Ravenscroft, we have that ready. You'll find a desk reserved in the reading room. If you need copies, we'll assist you."

Ewan thanked her and followed her directions. His route — echoing with whispers of the city's past—felt like stepping into another century. Dim, musty corridors stretched on, each lined with cabinets of files and drawers worn smooth by a century of hands that had passed over them. He found the narrow corridor "M" leading to a hushed, high-ceilinged reading room with rows of cabinets and tables. The air was cool and damp, carrying the weight of countless stories sealed in yellowed pages and faded ink. The walls seemed to hold secrets from ages past.

He found his desk, and there lay the files. Bound with thin ribbons and stamped with the unmistakable red wax seal of the archives, they seemed to contain more than mere facts. The seal was like a final barrier, a warning that what lay beyond was not only hidden by time but protected by ritual. Ewan's fingers hesitated momentarily before he broke the seal, undoing the ribbon and unfolding the brittle pages.

His time here was brief, barely enough to scratch the surface of what these files held. But a few words and lines he'd read—precognition records, prison logs, and witness statements—were enough to echo his grandfather's suspicions and fuel his drive to dig deeper. The documents spoke of a case marked by questionable evidence and coerced testimony—a police force eager to close the trial on Pasha Liffey, the first Black man to face the gallows in Scotland. Ewan knew he'd need to thoroughly review these records at home, where he could finally let the details unfold.

Emerging from the archives into the cold November dusk, the damp air settled like a chill straight through his coat. As he made his way toward the car park, the glow of Edinburgh's streetlights flickered on, casting long shadows across the wet pavement. The street was empty; save for a few lone figures huddling in scarves, faces turned down against the wind. Somewhere in the distance, the harsh caw of a crow cut through the silence, echoing off the stone buildings as if mocking his long hours in the archives.

The car park was barely lit, a tired, sprawling square littered with the leftovers of city life—crumpled fast-food wrappers, greasy paper bags, crushed beer cans glinting under the faint light. Autumn leaves were heaped in windblown drifts against the car park's edges, damp hedges tangled with the remnants of last night's meals and soggy receipts.

In the far corner, Ewan noticed a figure—a crow perched atop an abandoned shopping trolley. The bird's black feathers gleamed under the light, and its head tilted to the side, watching him with a beady, knowing eye. Around the trolley, other crows pecked at the cold leftovers of someone's discarded chips, jabbing their beaks into polystyrene cartons and ripping at crumpled sandwich wrappers. The lead crow on the trolley remained still, its gaze fixed on Ewan, a silent witness to the night's debris.

As he reached his car, the crows scattered briefly, wings flapping, before circling back to their feast. Ewan fumbled with his keys, the crow's stare lingering in his mind. It was as though the bird knew something, some piece of the puzzle he'd spent hours chasing in the archives. He slipped into the driver's seat and tossed the heavy bundle of files onto the passenger seat, their contents still begging for closer inspection.

Before turning the key, he reached for the glove compartment, pulling out an old, well-worn tape. The half-faded label bore the scrawl "Peter Gabriel - Bio." Ewan slid it into the cassette player, and the worn tape whirred to life. Familiar lyrics filtered through the speakers—

"September '77
Port Elizabeth weather is fine
It was business as usual
In police room 619
Oh Biko, Biko, because Biko
Oh Biko, Biko, because Biko
Yihla Moja, Yihla Moja
The man is dead—"

Peter Gabriel's haunting voice filled the quiet space of the car.

With the files beside him and Gabriel's voice echoing around him, Ewan's thoughts drifted to the work ahead. There remained much research to untangle in the wintry weeks ahead. As he pulled out of the parking lot, he felt the weight of it all—a story still unfinished, calling for him to dig deeper from the depths of history.

With his research complete, Ewan presented his findings to his editor, a conceptual pitch for a feature that could finally bring Pasha's story to light.

The office was a relic, just like the man who sat behind the cluttered desk. John "Mac" McAllister, known to his friends and enemies alike as simply Mac, ran his corner of the world with a style that was as outdated as it was effective. Cigarette smoke hung in the air, and walls, once white, were stained by decades of nicotine. A battered old Royal typewriter sat proudly on his desk, its keys worn smooth from years of service—a monument to a different time, a journalist's time. Even in 2005, Mac insisted

213

on copy handed to him on paper, and he wasn't shy about spiking a story with a satisfying "thunk" if it didn't cut the mustard.

Mac had a knack for making things happen, of getting stories into print. It was part of why Ewan respected him. For all his old-world quirks, Mac understood what sold, and he knew how to polish a pitch—even if he barked his criticism more than he praised. For writers who delivered, Mac was loyal; he had an almost magical way of getting his stringers' stories onto the front page.

The desk was chaos. Piles of paper—articles, press releases, news clippings—all competing for space, surrounding the editor. At the very edge of the desk, next to a glass ashtray filled with butts, stood the old spike, where rejected stories were still impaled with that deadly finality. Mac liked the finality of a story spiked. It was dead when something didn't cut, and Mac ensured the writers knew it.

As Ewan Ravenscroft II sat down across from him, the office was quiet except for the soft hum of the radiator in the corner. No bustling newsroom surrounded them—Mac ran a one-person band, keeping the dying art of old-school journalism alive. He didn't look up at first, busy flipping through a few sheets of paper, glancing at the bolded headings. Paper crinkling punctuated the silence before Mac finally looked up, squinting over his reading glasses.

"Pasha, huh?" Mac muttered, lighting another cigarette and taking a slow drag. His voice was rough. "Your grandfather, he covered that?"

Ewan nodded. "He did. In this case... there's something wrong with it, Mac. There's a lot that doesn't add up. Precognition records, identical witness statements, all of it feels staged."

Mac raised an eyebrow but remained silent, flipping through the typed sheets Ewan had handed him.

Then, with a sharp flick of his wrist, he tossed the sheets onto the desk. "No public interest. This is history Ravenscroft. People don't care about that shit. They want the now."

He reached over, impaled the sheets on the spike, and glanced back at Ewan. "There's more important shit out there to cover. Rumour has it the IPCC's about to make a statement on de Menezes." He let the name linger, seeing if Ewan would take the bait. "That Brazilian electrician they mistook for a terrorist, shot down at Stockwell station."

Mac paused, watching Ewan's reaction. "Police under fire, the big debate over lethal force—and the public are eating it up. Real-time, real news," he added.

Mac took a last drag on his cigarette, his eyes locked on Ewan as if daring him to protest. "If there's any truth to that announcement, you'd better be there to catch it." The click of his lighter as he lit another cigarette signalled the end of the conversation.

Ewan stood, the sting of rejection familiar but bitter. Mac did not believe in ghosts, but Ewan did. He could still feel the suitcase's weight, his grandfather's notes, and the unfinished story about Pasha's trial. But Mac was already deep into another file, his hands working through more stories that needed spiking or saving. For Mac, the past was a distraction, and today's weight always took precedence.

The December chill bit into him as Ewan stepped outside the offices onto the cold pavement. He was lost in thought, replaying Mac's words in his mind. His gaze lifted briefly to the grey sky, where a single black crow circled above, its feathers gleaming against the fading light. It drifted slowly down to land on a nearby lamppost, watching him. Ewan took one last look at the crow before turning and walking into the London streets, the weight of his unfinished story pressing against his chest.

THE CROW'S CALL

The Ladywell estate rose quietly against the dull Glasgow sky, its angular facades softened by the pale light of an overcast afternoon. Children's laughter rang out in the distance, their voices echoing off concrete walls. Somewhere, the rhythmic thud of a football hitting the pavement punctuated the stillness. Life here was unhurried, unaware of the history buried beneath it.

Ewan Ravenscroft stood on a small patch of green tucked between the estate's modern buildings. The grass, slick with rain, clung to his shoes as he shifted his weight. This patch had been left untouched during development—some said out of respect, others whispered of superstition. Either way, it had become a quiet anomaly. In this space, memory lingered like the low mist curling over the ground.

His breath hung in the cold air. He stared at the grass. Beneath this unassuming patch lay Pasha Liffey, Scotland's first and only Black man to face the gallows. No stone marked his grave. His name had faded from the city's memory, but standing here, Ewan felt the weight of his story pressing against him—a ghost demanding to be heard.

Crouching, he ran his fingers lightly over the damp earth. The grass was soft, yielding to his touch, but beneath it lay the cold, unyielding earth that had held Pasha for over a century.

The documents he'd uncovered were fresh in his mind—trial transcripts, coerced testimonies, and his grandfather's scribbled notes. Each detail chipped away at the story Scotland had accepted for over a hundred years. The evidence felt staged, the trial rushed, and the outcome predetermined. Yet, even with the truth emerging, Ewan wondered if it would ever matter. Would anyone care? Could Pasha's name rise from this ground, or would he remain a historical footnote?

A sharp caw broke his thoughts. Ewan looked up to see a crow perched on a skeletal branch above him, its feathers black as coal and gleaming in the pale light. Its head tilted, watching him with an unblinking gaze. The bird's presence felt deliberate.

He straightened, his boots sinking slightly into the wet ground as he stood. "It has to begin somewhere," he murmured, his voice low, more to himself than the crow.

The crow cawed again as if answering him before spreading its wings. The rush of air was loud in the quiet, and Ewan watched as it soared into the sky, its silhouette shrinking until it disappeared into the grey.

Ewan turned and began walking down the gravel path, leaving the green patch behind. But the image of that quiet square of grass stayed with him, a silent reminder of what was buried there—and what still needed to rise.

Around him, the Ladywell estate buzzed with life. Laughter and voices carried on the air, the modern world moving forward. Yet Ewan felt the past pulling at him, not as a weight but as a purpose. Pasha Liffey's story was not over, not yet. And as long as Ewan had breath in his body and ink in his pen, it never would be.

Let me share how Pasha's Journey came to life!

It all started with a simple curiosity. I took a DNA test a few years ago, hoping to learn more about my heritage. What I did not expect was to tumble headfirst into history. The results connected me to a sprawling family tree—a story I had never known. My grandfather, I discovered, left England in September 1899 to fight in the Boer War. He settled in South Africa, married a Boer woman, and began a new life. Intrigued, I started reading about the Boer War—its battles and the untold stories that lurked in its shadows.

One day, while scrolling through archival materials, I found a photograph that stopped me. It showed a group of African men delivering supplies to a British camp. Barefoot, unarmed, and leading wagons loaded with food and ammunition into the heart of the battlefield. Who were they? What were their stories? Why weren't they remembered? I needed to know more.

As I dug deeper, I uncovered the lives of tens of thousands of Africans recruited during the Boer War—not as soldiers, but as scouts, messengers, labourers, and runners. These men were the lifeblood of the war effort, indispensable yet treated as entirely expendable. The runners, in particular, fascinated me. These men threaded through enemy lines, delivering messages and intelligence, their bravery holding the war together. Yet their names have largely been erased from history. Their courage and untold stories stayed with me, and I began sketching the outline of a novel—a book I intended to call *The Runners*.

But somewhere in the middle of countless hours spent chasing rabbit holes, tangents, and more obscure leads than I care to admit, I stumbled upon a newspaper cutting that stopped me in my tracks. It detailed the execution, on November 14, 1905, of Pasha Liffey, a young Basuto from Mafeteng—the first (and only) African to be executed in Scotland. That one discovery made all the late nights and caffeine-fuelled searches worthwhile.

The clipping revealed that Pasha had claimed to be a runner during the Boer War. A runner? For British troops? Other accounts suggested he might have worked as a groom for an officer named Fraser. And yet, there was more: 350 men from the 2nd Battalion Scottish Rifles—the Cameronians—had signed a petition pleading for clemency, believing in his service during the war. These fragments of his life raised more questions than they answered.

At the time, I did not know whether Pasha had been at Mafeking or elsewhere. I knew his story deserved to be told, and the more I pieced it together, the more I realised it was more compelling than the broader narrative of *The Runners* I had initially imagined. If there is any poetic licence in this book, it lies in Pasha's role as a runner at the Siege of Mafeking. He could just as quickly have been a groom or a messenger anywhere else in South Africa during the Boer War.

His life took an unexpected turn when he arrived in Ipswich on April 12, 1891, at the age of eleven, under the care of Douglas Henry Fraser. For nearly seven years, he lived in England, working as a groom, until he returned to South Africa on April

10, 1898. Less than a year later, he boarded the SS Goth in March 1899, part of the Savage South Africa show at Earl's Court from May until October 1899. From there, his life becomes a tightly woven timeline. In October 1899, he attempted suicide in Northampton after a breakup. By March 10, 1900, he was arrested for drunkenness in Braunston, Northamptonshire. If he served in the Boer War, his only opportunity was between late October 1899 and early February 1900—a narrow window, but not impossible.

By 1905, Pasha's life had taken a tragic turn. On August 11, Mary Jane Welsh was murdered in Larkhall, Scotland. Witnesses claimed to have seen Pasha fleeing the scene. Despite the ambiguities in the evidence, his trial was swift, and the outcome was inevitable. On November 14, 1905, Pasha was hanged at Duke Street Prison in Glasgow.

This book is my attempt to honour lives like Pasha's and remember the people who shaped history in the shadows of the Empire. It is about shining a light on the voices that history has tried to silence. Through Pasha's Journey, I want to inspire you to question our inherited stories and bring light to the voices that have been ignored for far too long. The past is not behind us—it's there for us to uncover.

As you turn the following pages, you will find mini-biographies of the key characters in this story. These are designed to help separate fact from fiction and provide a deeper understanding of the people who played a role in Pasha's world.

You will also discover a timeline of significant events, tracing Pasha's life alongside performances of the Savage South Africa show and critical moments in history. This timeline is backed by archival records, newspaper articles, and meticulous research, ensuring every date and event is rooted in fact.

—Dennis

Also, Now I need to breathe life into *The Runners* and perhaps sketch and write the worlds of Savage South Africa and Texas Jack. These stories deserve their place in the spotlight.

STILL MORE TO READ

At about the same time young Pasha was making his way to Fraser's Trading Store in Liphiring, another story was taking shape, some 890 kilometres to the northeast, in the wilds of Matabeleland. Here, under a punishing sky and amidst thorn trees and shifting sands, stood Johan Colenbrander, a man as multifaceted as the landscape. He was an adventurer and a cattle trader, a loyalist and a maverick, a crack shot and a shrewd businessman—all wrapped up in one broad-shouldered package. His companion, James Grant, a Scottish whisky distiller with a taste for Africa's beauty and grit, was no less colourful. Together, they were on the trail of big game, their rifles slung over their shoulders, eyes peeled for whatever thundered through the brush.

As they tracked, their boots kicking up the ochre dust, they stumbled upon two young boys—skinny, hungry-eyed children clutching each other for warmth in the fading sun. They were with an old cattle herder and his wife, who had crossed paths with Colenbrander for reasons lost to the dry air and shifting fortunes. Grant, known for a soft spot beneath his grizzled demeanour, offered a solution, a promise of a different life for one of the boys. And so it was that young Biawa, a boy of about eight, left his home and set off for a land of mist and mystery, far removed from the thorny scrublands he had known.

Biawa arrived in Rothes, a quiet Scottish town nestled along the River Spey, known for its whisky and football pitch. Here, he earned a new name—Mak—and a life of strange, sturdy stability with it. He learned the Scots' rhythms and took to the football field with fierce determination, soon becoming Rothes Victoria's unlikely but dependable goalkeeper. He was no longer just seen as Grant's servant but as Mak, the young African with a soft brogue and a steady presence.

Then came the call of war. It was 1916, and Mak, now twenty-six, enlisted at Fort George in the British Army, the Northamptonshire Regiment. Officially, regulations did not permit men like him to serve beside white soldiers. Still, a letter from Major Grant made an exception. And so, Biawa Makalaga was swept into the heat of the Middle East with the Mesopotamia Expeditionary Force, sent to fight the Turks under a sun that burned like judgment. For his service, he would be awarded the British War Medal and the Victory Medal—tokens of a world far removed from Rothes or Matabeleland, symbols of a story few could grasp.

After the war, he returned to the life he had left behind at Glen Grant House. He resumed his role with a quiet, steady loyalty that did not go unnoticed. He was still a fixture on the football pitch, a figure sipping his half-time tea and watching the younger men kick and sweat the way he once had. When Major Grant passed in 1931, he ensured that Mak would be looked after, provided he remained "respectful and sober." And so, he did, working for the Major's daughter Mary, living out his days in the place that had, somehow, become his own.

On January 4, 1972, Biawa "Mak" Makalaga died, leaving his life savings—£36.11s, a gun, a fishing rod, and a saw—to Rothes FC. It was a modest sum, but the gesture meant more than the money. In Rothes, Mak was no longer just "the African" or "the servant." He had become something more enduring—a part of the town, one of its own.

Even now, Rothes speaks of him. Some claim to see his ghost near the distillery, a lone figure cloaked in the mist, watching over the town that became his unlikely home. They say he walks with a steady stride, as if still patrolling the grounds of Glen Grant House, his footsteps echoing softly against the stone.

Others whisper of his silhouette near the football pitch at twilight, standing by the goalposts, watching the young lads play as though keeping a silent vigil. Whether real or imagined, these sightings carry a weight of quiet reverence, a testament to the life of a boy who crossed an ocean and became part of Rothes' soul.

Mak's story endures in the tales of those who remember him—not as an outsider but as one of their own. He reminds us of a world that once spanned thorny scrublands, frosted fields, and a man who belonged to both. Perhaps, even now, in the gentle mist that blankets the River Spey, Biawa Makalaga lingers—part memory, part spirit—forever at home in two worlds.

The "Cast" in Pasha's Journey

Pasha Liffey (1880 – 1905)

Solomon Tshekisho Plaatje (1876–1932)

Sol Plaatje was a South African intellectual, journalist, and political activist. During the Siege of Mafeking (1899–1900), a pivotal event in the Second Boer War, Plaatje served as a court interpreter and documented his experiences in a diary that offered a unique perspective on the conflict.

Born in the Orange Free State, Plaatje was multilingual and fluent in several languages, including Tswana, English, and Dutch. His linguistic skills led to his appointment as a court interpreter in Mafeking, where he witnessed the 217-day siege firsthand. Throughout this period, he meticulously recorded daily events, providing insights into the lives of both the besieged residents and the African population's role during the conflict.

Plaatje's diary, later published as "Mafeking Diary: A Black Man's View of a White Man's War," is notable for its detailed accounts of the siege and its critique of colonial attitudes. His writings challenge the prevailing narratives of the time, highlighting the contributions and experiences of black South Africans, which were often overlooked in mainstream accounts.

Beyond his work during the siege, Plaatje became a prominent figure in South African history. He was a founding member and the first General Secretary of the South African Native National Congress (SANNC), later the African National Congress (ANC). His literary contributions include the novel "Mhudi" and translations of Shakespeare's works into Tswana, reflecting his commitment to preserving and promoting African languages and culture.

Sol Plaatje's legacy endures through his writings and advocacy for black South Africans' rights. His diary remains a vital historical document, offering a nuanced perspective on the complexities of the Second Boer War and the broader colonial context.

Peter Kushana Lobengula

Peter Kushana Lobengula strode into the pages of history with a story as complex as the continent he hailed from. Claiming to be the son of King Lobengula, the last ruler of the Matabele people, Peter's life was a tapestry of triumph and tragedy, woven against the backdrop of colonial spectacle and Victorian rigidity. Whether his royal lineage was fact or fabrication remains an enigma. Still, one thing is sure: his journey captivated and unsettled the world equally.

Born amidst the turmoil of a crumbling kingdom, Peter grew up in the shadow of the Matabele Wars, where his father's realm fell to Cecil Rhodes's insatiable imperial ambitions. By the time Peter set foot in Britain, the Ndebele people's sovereignty had been reduced to a memory, their struggle immortalised not by their telling but in the lurid displays of imperial pageantry.

1899, Peter joined Frank Fillis's "Savage South Africa" show. This spectacle brought the drama of colonial conquest to the heart of London. Staged at Earl's Court, the production reenacted battles from the Matabele Wars, with Peter cast as a living symbol of a defeated Empire. He quickly became a star attraction, his presence lending both intrigue and authenticity to Fillis's imperial fantasy. Champagne toasts with the Prince of Wales cemented his celebrity. Yet, his life offstage revealed the churning undercurrents of a society grappling with race, power, and spectacle.

During this time, Peter's path crossed with Kitty Jewell, a 23-year-old Cornishwoman whose life had already brushed against Africa during her father's prospecting days in Bloemfontein. Some say their romance began on South African soil; others insist it blossomed amidst the clamour of the Earl's Court. Either way, their union caused an uproar. Kitty, drawn to Peter's charisma and tales of Africa, found herself enraptured. At the same time, the British tabloids gleefully exploited their engagement as both scandal and sensation. Their marriage in 1899 was a rare act of defiance in an era bound by the shackles of racial prejudice.

Yet the weight of public scrutiny—and perhaps deeper incompatibilities—proved too great. Kitty accused Peter of theft, a charge that led to their bitter divorce in 1901. Kitty emigrated to America, leaving behind the storm of their union. At the same time, Peter remained in England, where the limelight faded into a quiet existence. He worked as a miner in Salford, far removed from the glittering notoriety of Earl's Court.

In his later years, Peter married an Irishwoman named Catherine and raised a family, though his royal claims persisted. In an unexpected turn, he successfully argued his right to vote in local elections, invoking his lineage as the son of King Lobengula. It was a small, defiant gesture in a life shaped by much larger forces. Sadly, tuberculosis claimed him in 1913, ending a life that had navigated the extremes of fame, labour, and quiet dignity.

Peter Kushana Lobengula remains an intriguing figure. His story mirrors the tensions of his time—between Empire and identity, spectacle and survival. Whether celebrated as a prince or remembered as a miner, his life defied easy categorisation, challenging the world to reckon with the humanity behind the headlines.

Florence Kate "Kitty" Jewell

Florence Kate "Kitty" Jewell, a British piano teacher, became a notable figure in the late 19th century due to her relationship with Peter Kushana Lobengula, a performer in the "Savage South Africa" show. Their romance unfolded against intense public and media scrutiny, reflecting Victorian Britain's rigid racial attitudes.

The couple likely met in Bloemfontein, South Africa, though the details of their early relationship remain unclear. By 1899, Kitty had moved to London, settling near Earl's Court—the venue for the "Savage South Africa" show where Lobengula performed. Their plans to marry in August of that year were met with public outrage, mainly because interracial relationships were heavily stigmatised. The press sensationalised their love story, portraying it as scandalous, and Kitty's mother even attempted to block the marriage by claiming her daughter was insane.

Despite these challenges, Kitty and Lobengula quietly married at the Holborn Register Office on February 28, 1900. Unfortunately, their marriage quickly turned sour. Kitty accused

Lobengula of adultery and cruelty, leading to their divorce in 1902. After that, Kitty's life became somewhat obscure, with little information about her subsequent years.

Kitty's relationship with Lobengula serves as a lens into the racial and social tensions of the era. The hostility they faced highlights the challenges that interracial couples endured during a time dominated by colonial attitudes and strict social hierarchies. Their story also reflects the emergence of tabloid journalism, which thrived on sensationalism and scandal, shaping public perception of such relationships.

Texas Jack Jr.

Texas Jack Jr. (c. 1860–1905) was an American entertainer who adopted the name of his rescuer and mentor, Texas Jack Omohundro. His birth name remains unknown, but Omohundro, a renowned scout and cowboy, profoundly influenced his life. After being saved from a perilous situation, he took on the name Texas Jack Jr., honouring his benefactor.

Under Omohundro's guidance, Texas Jack Jr. entered the world of Wild West entertainment, establishing himself as a sharpshooter, trick rider, and performer. By the late 1890s, he had gained international recognition, performing in Wild West shows that showcased his talents beyond the American frontier.

In 1899, Texas Jack Jr. joined the "Savage South Africa" show, where he reenacted historical battles between British colonial forces and Indigenous African warriors. Notably, he portrayed Frederick Russell Burnham, a survivor of the Shangani Patrol battle. This theatrical production brought African colonial history to European audiences and inspired one of the earliest war films, "Major Wilson's Last Stand."

Following the success of the "Savage South Africa" show, Texas Jack Jr. created "Texas Jack's Wild West Show & Circus" in South Africa. His performances combined elements of the American Wild West with African settings, featuring sharpshooting stunts and dramatic reenactments. His international fame helped spread the mythos of the American West to audiences unfamiliar with the frontier lifestyle.

Texas Jack Jr. passed away in Kroonstad, South Africa, in 1905. He was survived by his common-law wife, Lyle Marr, who had performed alongside him as a sharpshooter in his shows. Despite his death far from his homeland, Texas Jack Jr.'s influence on American and South African entertainment persisted long after his passing.

His career illustrated the global reach of the American frontier myth and its enduring appeal to audiences worldwide.

The SS Goth

The SS Goth was far more than a mere steamship; it was a vessel of the Empire, pivotal in transporting soldiers, supplies, and spectacles during the height of British colonial expansion. Built in 1893 for the Union Steamship Company, the SS Goth epitomised the dual-purpose functionality of its time—serving as a workhorse of war and a vehicle for cultural export.

Designed for efficiency and reliability, the SS Goth operated primarily between Southampton and Cape Town, a vital artery of the British Empire in southern Africa. It was equipped to carry passengers, livestock, military supplies, and colonial personnel. During the Second Boer War (1899–1902), the ship ferried British troops and equipment to the frontlines, becoming an essential cog in the machinery of war that would reshape the region's socio-political landscape. Its voyages symbolised Britain's commitment to consolidating its influence in South Africa, often at the expense of local populations.

However, the SS Goth's legacy extends beyond its military service. In 1899, it was uniquely hired for a very different mission—transporting the performers and animals of Frank Fillis's " Savage South Africa" show to Britain. This travelling spectacle sought to bring the drama of colonial conflicts and African "exoticism" to European audiences. On this voyage, the SS Goth carried not only men, women, and children from southern Africa but also elephants, lions, horses, and other animals, all part of the show's theatrical reenactments of battles such as the Shangani Patrol. The ship became a floating microcosm of the Empire, a space where lives and narratives are intertwined in the service of war and entertainment.

Transporting these performers and animals highlights the ship's multifaceted role in the colonial enterprise, blending commerce, culture, and conflict. For the performers, this journey represented a dislocation—many were thrust into a world that would commodify their identities and traditions for Western audiences. For the animals, it was a brutal reminder of the human exploitation of the natural world, with their inclusion in the spectacle symbolising dominion over both people and nature.

Despite the maritime challenges of the time, the SS Goth gained a reputation for dependable service, completing its voyages with minimal incidents. Yet, like many ships of its era, it was eventually outpaced by newer, more advanced vessels. The SS Goth faded into obsolescence as the early 20th century ushered in an era of rapid technological progress.

Its story, however, endures as a testament to the intertwined forces of Empire, entertainment, and colonial expansion. The SS Goth was more than a steamship; it was a vessel that carried not only passengers and cargo but also the weight of an imperial legacy, connecting continents and shaping the narratives of a tumultuous era.

"Savage South Africa" was a theatrical spectacle that stormed Britain in the late 19th century. Debuting in 1899 at Earl's Court, this show dramatized British colonial conflicts in Africa. It was created by South African showman Frank Fillis, who knew how to exploit the British public's fascination with adventure and the Empire during intense conflict.

The production featured over two hundred African performers, mainly from the Zulu, Matabele, and Basuto communities, along with British soldiers and Boers. While the show aimed to create an immersive experience with live animals and authentic props, it also reinforced harmful colonial narratives. Performers were often treated as living exhibits, echoing the era's troubling fascination with "human zoos."

The spectacle catered to a British audience eager for excitement, portraying African warriors as "savage" in stark contrast to the "civilised" British forces. While it celebrated the physical prowess of its African participants, it ultimately reduced their identities to mere entertainment, perpetuating racial stereotypes and romanticising the violence of colonialism.

The portrayal of the Shangani Patrol, with Texas Jack Jr. playing Frederick Russell Burnham, exemplified this troubling dynamic. While the reenactment captured attention, it glorified British military dominance while obscuring the resilience and agency of African people.

Despite its commercial success, "Savage South Africa" faced criticism for its exploitative nature. Many African performers endured harsh conditions and received minimal compensation, highlighting the broader system of exploitation inherent in colonial entertainment. The tensions within the performances exposed the contradictions faced by British audiences, who consumed narratives of African resistance while simultaneously celebrating imperial conquests.

As political tensions escalated around the Boer War and the novelty of such exhibitions began to wane, the show's popularity declined. Fillis eventually returned to South Africa, but the legacy of "Savage South Africa" lingered, influencing how British and European audiences perceived Africa and its people.

In retrospect, "Savage South Africa" is a complex artefact of its time. While it captivated audiences, it also entrenched harmful stereotypes and commodified the very cultures it claimed to represent.

Frank E. Fillis: The Showman of Empire

Frank E. Fillis (1857–1921) was a South African showman whose large-scale performances, including the controversial "Savage South Africa" show, epitomised the intersection of entertainment, imperialism, and exploitation in the name of Empire. While achieving commercial success, Fillis' work also perpetuated harmful racial stereotypes and glorified colonial domination, leaving a legacy as contentious as it was influential.

Born in Yorkshire, England, Fillis began his career in the circus industry, honing his craft as a showman and promoter. His move to South Africa in the late 19th century provided the literal and figurative stage for his most ambitious productions. There, he capitalised on the colonial fervour of the time, staging performances that dramatized British imperial adventures, often at the expense of the dignity and autonomy of indigenous peoples.

Fillis became known for blending circus-style entertainment with reenactments of African culture and colonial history. His productions prominently featured African performers, but their roles were framed within narratives that glorified British conquest. Rather than celebrating the rich complexities of African cultures, Fillis' shows presented a distorted version of those cultures, reinforcing the racist ideologies underpinning imperial rule.

The pinnacle of Fillis' career came in 1899, with the debut of "Savage South Africa" at London's Earl's Court. This ambitious production involved over two hundred African performers, including Matabele and Zulu nations members, and live animals such as elephants and lions. The show reenacted battles from the Matabele Wars and the Anglo-Zulu War, portraying British forces as heroic and civilised while casting African resistance as savage and chaotic. In reality, the show was a spectacle, and a form of propaganda designed to justify colonial expansion and domination.

While the show enjoyed significant commercial success, it was deeply exploitative. The African performers were often viewed as little more than living exhibits in what amounted to a "human zoo." Stripped of their cultural agency, they were forced to reenact scenes of their subjugation for the amusement of Western audiences. The use of real animals and warriors added to the exotic allure. Still, it also underscored the dehumanising practices of the era, reducing vibrant cultures and living beings to commodities of imperial entertainment.

Fillis' productions, while groundbreaking in their scale, were emblematic of the racial ideologies and exploitative practices that defined colonial exhibitions. His shows not only entertained but also reinforced a narrative of British superiority, contributing to the systemic dehumanisation of African peoples in the global imagination.

Frank Fillis died in 1921, leaving a legacy that continues to spark critical examination. His work stands as a stark reminder of how entertainment has historically been used to legitimise the Empire, perpetuate racism, and commodify cultural identities. While his name is remembered for his showmanship, it also symbolises the darker realities of colonial exploitation and the enduring impact of imperialist narratives in shaping perceptions of Africa and its peoples.

Rev. Édouard Jacottet

Rev. Édouard Jacottet (1858–1920) was a French missionary whose work in Basutoland (modern-day Lesotho) reflects the complex and often fraught legacy of missionary activities during the colonial era. Sent to Thaba-Bossiou by the Société des Missions Évangéliques de Paris in 1884, Jacottet's efforts were deeply intertwined with the broader dynamics of imperialism and cultural disruption.

Jacottet was a linguist and scholar recognised for his contributions to studying and preserving the Sesotho language. His translations of Christian texts into Sesotho aimed to promote Christianity among the Basotho people. However, this work often came at the expense of local spiritual traditions, reframing them within a European religious framework that marginalised indigenous beliefs. His publication Litsomo tsa Basotho (Legends of the Basotho) preserved oral traditions but also reinterpreted them through a colonial lens, reflecting the paternalistic attitudes of his time.

As a missionary, Jacottet worked to impose European religious and cultural ideals, often disregarding Basotho's autonomy and rich spiritual heritage. While he viewed his efforts as a path toward education and salvation, they frequently aligned with the broader colonial project of eroding local identities and reinforcing European dominance.

Jacottet's life ended abruptly and tragically in 1920 when he was poisoned at the Morija mission station. The circumstances surrounding his death remain unclear, but they highlight the underlying tensions between missionaries and local populations, as well as the broader risks faced by those operating within the volatile dynamics of colonialism.

The legacy of Rev. Édouard Jacottet is a complex one. On one hand, his work contributed to documenting and preserving African languages and cultural traditions. On the other, it exemplified the exploitative nature of missionary activities that sought to reshape societies in the image of European ideals. His life and work invite critical reflection on the impacts of missionary efforts during the colonial period, urging us to consider the voices and perspectives of those who resisted cultural and spiritual subjugation.

The Fraser Brothers

Donald and Douglas Fraser were British traders whose activities in Basutoland (modern-day Lesotho) during the late 19th century exemplify the economic and cultural shifts imposed by colonialism. Born in Ipswich, England, to a family of wool merchants, the brothers carried their mercantile expertise to southern Africa, establishing their first trading store in Liphiring in 1877. Their enterprise grew to dominate local commerce, embedding themselves deeply in the colonial economic framework.

The Fraser brothers are most notably associated with popularising the Basotho blanket, a now-iconic symbol of Lesotho's national identity. Initially, the Basotho wore traditional animal-skin karosses, but the introduction of imported blankets marked a significant cultural transition. While the blankets brought practical benefits, their widespread adoption illustrates the profound influence of colonial trade practices in reshaping indigenous traditions. The Frasers capitalised on this shift, positioning their products as indispensable while profiting from the dependency they cultivated within Basotho society.

Their operations coincided with turbulent times, including the Gun War (1880–1881), sparked by British efforts to disarm the Basotho. The Frasers' role during this conflict highlights the exploitative nature of their enterprise. Supplying goods to both sides of the war, they ensured their economic gain amidst the chaos, consolidating power while the Basotho fought to retain their autonomy. This opportunism underscored the broader patterns of colonial commerce, where profit often outweighed ethical considerations.

As Frasers Ltd expanded, its network of stores became a cornerstone of colonial dominance in Basutoland. While their goods met practical needs, the Frasers' economic strategies reinforced systems of exploitation and control, aligning their success with the broader colonial project. The dependency fostered by their business model exemplified how trade and commerce were wielded as tools of imperial influence.

The Fraser brothers' legacy is as complex as it is contentious. The Basotho blanket, now a cherished cultural emblem, serves as both a reminder of colonial influence and a symbol of resilience, repurposed by the Basotho to assert their identity. The

Fraser brothers' story invites critical reflection on the intersections of trade, culture, and power in colonial contexts, highlighting commerce's profound and often exploitative impacts in reshaping indigenous societies.

The Crow

The crow is enigmatic, embodying mystery, intelligence, and transformation. Its profound presence is woven into the myths and beliefs of countless cultures. The crow commands reverence and fear, serving as a powerful messenger between realms, a cunning trickster, and a guardian of ancient wisdom.

In various traditions, the crow is believed to carry crucial messages between the physical and spiritual worlds, whispering secrets of the unseen to those attuned to its call. It acts as a guide, navigating the delicate balance between life and death, with its appearance often heralding change, transition, or profound truths yearning to be unveiled. While some perceive it as a harbinger of forewarnings, others recognise it as a devoted protector, watching over souls' journeys as they transcend this earthly existence. Legends often portray the crow as a trickster, adept at using its wit and cunning to outsmart those who attempt to manipulate fate. It thrives on intelligence and adaptability, imparting lessons through deception and unexpected insights.

In other narratives, it emerges as a bearer of sacred knowledge entrusted with the mysteries of creation, destiny, and the eternal cycles of existence. Throughout the ages, the crow has oscillated between fear and reverence, standing resolutely at the intersection of the known and the unknown.

Whether viewed as a herald of prophecy, a guardian of ancestral wisdom, or a guide through the shadows, it remains a powerful symbol of transformation, fate, and the eternal dance between darkness and light. Within the depths of its dark wings lies an echo of the past and the promise of what is yet to unfold.

F.Z.S. Peregrino

F.Z.S. Peregrino, born in Accra, Ghana 1851, emerged as a significant voice in Pan-African journalism and activism during the late 19th and early 20th centuries. After completing his early education, he relocated to England, where he initially worked in a steel foundry before diving into journalism. His passion for advocating for the rights of Black individuals led him to the United States, where he published The Spectator in Albany, New York.

Inspired by the ideals of the Pan-African movement, Peregrino returned to Cape Town after attending the first Pan-African Congress in 1900. He founded The South African Spectator, the first newspaper explicitly aimed at a Black readership there. Through this publication, he sought to foster pride and unity among people of colour, emphasising the importance of collective identity in the face of systemic racism.

Peregrino believed in building bridges between African and Coloured communities, advocating for their shared rights and interests. He condemned any attempts to create divisions, recognising that solidarity was crucial for challenging colonial oppression. His editorial work was marked by a commitment to social justice, using his platform to highlight the struggles and aspirations of marginalised groups.

In addition to his journalistic endeavours, Peregrino played a vital role in establishing organisations that served the needs of the District Six community in Cape Town. He founded the Coloured Men's Protectorate and Political Association and the Coloured People's Vigilance Association, which aimed to extend political rights and protections to all Black South Africans.

Peregrino's influence extended beyond traditional media; he also initiated the "Stone Meetings," an open forum for political discussion held near Table Mountain. These gatherings, which continued for over two decades, provided a space for residents to engage in meaningful dialogue about their rights and the social issues affecting their lives.

Despite facing significant challenges, including racial discrimination and political resistance, Peregrino remained steadfast in his commitment to uplifting his community. His efforts laid the groundwork for burgeoning Black consciousness among Coloured people and their regional organisations.

Peregrino passed away in 1919, but his legacy endures. He is remembered not only for his contributions to journalism but also for his unwavering dedication to the cause of equality and justice in South Africa. His life and work continues to inspire those who seek to confront colonialism's legacies and strive for a more inclusive society.

The Gwelo Coach

The Gwelo Coach is a complex artefact in the history of colonial transportation. It is emblematic of both the harsh realities of imperial expansion and the narratives often overlooked in the glorification of colonialism. Originally built to traverse the rugged terrain of Southern Rhodesia, now Zimbabwe, the coach facilitated the movement of settlers seeking wealth and opportunity at the expense of Indigenous populations.

Historically, the Gwelo Coach became notorious when Matabele warriors attacked it during the First Matabele War in March 1896. This ambush near the Shangani River exposed the violent tensions between British settlers and the Matabele people, who fiercely resisted colonial encroachment. Such resistance was not just a reaction to invasion but a declaration of the Matabele's sovereignty and a rejection of the colonial narrative that sought to erase their culture and autonomy.

Later, the Gwelo Coach was exported to the "Savage South Africa" exhibition in London, where it became a prop to entertain audiences with a romanticised view of Africa. In this context, the coach was a tool of colonial spectacle, reinforcing harmful stereotypes while glossing over the exploitation and suffering of indigenous peoples.

While the Gwelo Coach may have captured audiences' imagination, it also serves as a reminder of colonialism's darker aspects—the systemic oppression and dehumanisation of the very cultures it purported to represent. Its legacy invites critical reflection on the narratives of adventure and discovery that often overshadow the voices of those who resisted colonial domination, highlighting the urgent need for a more inclusive and truthful understanding of history.

Wilson's Last Stand

Wilson's Last Stand is a pivotal episode in the First Matabele War of 1896, occurring in Southern Rhodesia, now Zimbabwe. Named after Major Allan Wilson, this confrontation is often portrayed in colonial narratives as a heroic defence, but it also highlights the brutal reality of imperial expansion and the fierce resistance of the Matabele people.

As the British Empire sought to assert its dominance in Southern Africa, tensions escalated dramatically between settlers and the indigenous Matabele, led by King Lobengula. The Matabele fiercely resisted colonial encroachment, fighting for their land, identity, and way of life. This resistance resulted in violent conflicts often misrepresented in colonial histories, failing to recognise Matabele's struggle against invasion legitimacy.

In early 1896, Major Wilson and his thirty-four men embarked on a reconnaissance mission in Matabele territory. They were ambushed and surrounded by a more significant force of Matabele warriors near the Shangani River. Despite being heavily outnumbered, Wilson and his men took a defensive stance, preparing for an attack that stemmed from the Matabele's desire to protect their homeland.

The battle that ensued was marked by desperation and resilience. While Wilson and his troops fought valiantly, they were ultimately overwhelmed. All of Wilson's men were killed, and Major Wilson himself perished, a tragic outcome that has often been romanticised in colonial discourse. His death, rather than symbolising sacrifice for the Empire, represents the cost of imperialism on both sides—the loss of life, culture, and autonomy.

While noted in colonial circles, this event also underscores the fierce resistance of the Matabele. Wilson's Last Stand reminds us of the complexities of colonial conflicts in Southern Africa and highlights the bravery of those who fought to defend their land against colonial oppression.

Savage South Africa

"Savage South Africa", created by South African showman Frank Fillis, was a large-scale theatrical production that debuted at London's Earl's Court in 1899 as part of the Greater Britain Exhibition. This exhibition, celebrating Britain's imperial power, epitomised the nation's fascination with its colonies and the desire to glorify the Empire on a global stage. Running for six months, from May to October, the show attracted over a million visitors, including members of the British aristocracy, military figures, and the general public, all eager to glimpse the so-called "savage" lands of the Empire.

The production was both a spectacle and a statement, blending reenactments of colonial battles with cultural displays designed to reinforce British narratives of conquest and superiority. At its core were reenactments of conflicts such as the Anglo-Zulu War and the Matabele Wars, particularly the famous "Major Wilson's Last Stand," a dramatization of the doomed Shangani Patrol. The show presented British forces as heroic agents of civilisation. At the same time, African resistance was depicted as chaotic and savage, fitting neatly into the imperial propaganda of the time.

"Savage South Africa" featured over two hundred African performers, including members of the Matabele, Zulu, and Basuto nations, many of whom had been recruited—or coerced—into participating. Alongside them were European actors and a menagerie of live animals, including elephants, lions, and horses, which added to the spectacle. Including African performers and animals lent the show an air of authenticity. Still, it came at a great human and ethical cost. The performers, displaced from their homes, were subjected to gruelling schedules and forced to perform stereotypes that dehumanised them and commodified their cultures.

The show was not an isolated phenomenon but part of a broader movement celebrating Britain's Empire, often called "Greater Britain." The exhibition showcased the colonies as lands of opportunity and resources, with shows like "Savage South Africa" serving as entertainment and imperial propaganda. It reinforced the idea that British rule was inevitable and beneficial—a narrative eagerly consumed by audiences living at the height of the Empire.

The production drew crowds from across British society, from working-class families seeking cheap entertainment to upper-class elites who saw it as an educational insight into the Empire. Among the attendees were members of the royal family, including the Prince of Wales, who raised a champagne toast with the show's African performers during one notable event. The show's exotic allure, dramatic battle scenes, and live animals ensured its popularity, cementing its place as one of the most successful spectacles of the era.

After its six-month run at the Greater Britain Exhibition, "Savage South Africa" embarked on an extensive tour across the United Kingdom and Ireland, extending its performances for an additional year and a half. The production brought its spectacle to cities and towns such as Salford, where it was advertised for a three-week run in 1900. However, the extended tour was not without challenges. As the Second Boer War escalated, public interest in the dramatizations of colonial battles began to wane, overshadowed by the grim realities of the ongoing conflict. By January 1900, the show faced financial difficulties, leading to cancellations in some locations due to declining ticket sales. Despite these setbacks, Fillis adapted by reducing the production scale and continuing the tour with a more petite troupe, which included prominent performers like Peter Lobengula. This smaller iteration of "Savage South Africa" regained popularity in certain areas, particularly in regions less directly affected by the war.

Despite its initial success, "Savage South Africa" faced criticism for its exploitative nature. The practice of presenting humans as part of the spectacle drew comparisons to "human zoos," and certain humanitarian and religious groups condemned the dehumanising treatment of African performers. Debates in Parliament highlighted the ethical concerns surrounding such exhibitions. However, these objections were often overshadowed by the show's commercial appeal and the public's appetite for imperial spectacle.

Supporters of the show, including colonial officials and military figures, saw "Savage South Africa" as a valuable tool for promoting the Empire. It presented Britain as a benevolent power, bringing order and civilisation to distant lands. The involvement of African performers was framed as a cultural exchange. In reality, it was a stark illustration of colonial exploitation. The show also aligned with the burgeoning popularity of cinematic depictions of war, with its reenactments inspiring one of the earliest war films, Major Wilson's Last Stand.

The show finally concluded in 1901, leaving behind a complex legacy. It solidified the template for imperial exhibitions, combining entertainment with propaganda to reinforce the racial and cultural hierarchies underpinning colonialism. For many African performers, the experience was dislocation and alienation, their roles in the spectacle reducing them to objects of curiosity rather than individuals with agency and rich cultural histories.

Today, "Savage South Africa" stands as a symbol of the exploitative intersection of entertainment and Empire. It highlights how colonial powers commodified human lives and cultures to justify domination. While it captivated audiences at the time, it now serves as a critical reminder of the enduring consequences of imperialism and the narratives that continue to shape perceptions of Africa and its peoples.

Joseph 'Joe' Rosenthal (1864–1946) was a pioneering British cinematographer whose innovative work in early war and travel filmmaking left an indelible mark on the history of cinema. He trained as a pharmaceutical chemist. However, his career path took a decisive turn in late 1897 when he joined the Continental Commerce Company, the London agents for Edison films, at the suggestion of his sister, Alice Rosenthal, who served as the company's sales manager. His exceptional skill in photography quickly earned him a role as a camera operator.

In 1898, the Continental Commerce Company was rebranded as the Warwick Trading Company, under which Rosenthal embarked on filming assignments across the UK, Germany, the Netherlands, and South Africa. A pivotal moment in his career came with the outbreak of the Second Boer War in October 1899. Dispatched to Natal in January 1900, Rosenthal used the cutting-edge Biograph camera, known for its high-quality images, to document British military operations. His footage vividly captured troops marching, fording rivers, and taking Boer prisoners, providing audiences back home with a dramatic glimpse of the war.

Although much of Rosenthal's work focused on actual events, he occasionally staged scenes to compensate for the challenges of filming combat in real-time—a necessity given the constraints of contemporary equipment, military censorship, and the guerrilla tactics employed by the Boers. One notable example is A Skirmish with the Boers near Kimberley (1900), a staged battle featuring British cavalry designed to convey the intensity of the conflict. Despite these limitations, Rosenthal's dedication to his craft enabled him to produce a compelling visual record of the war, culminating in his documentation of the

British flag being raised in Pretoria on June 5, 1900, symbolising a significant turning point in the campaign.

Rosenthal's use of the Biograph camera, a cutting-edge technology of his time, elevated the technical quality of his films. With its large format and precision, this camera underscored his role as a pioneer in bringing war and travel imagery to life. His work during the Boer War solidified his reputation as one of the foremost cinematographers of his time, blending innovation with storytelling to capture the complexities of Empire and conflict.

William Kennedy Laurie Dickson

William Kennedy Laurie Dickson (1860–1935) was a British cinematographer, inventor, and filmmaker whose innovations shaped the foundation of early cinema. Born in Brittany, France, to Scottish parents, Dickson spent much of his early life in the United States, where he worked with Thomas Edison to develop the Kinetoscope and Kinetograph. These groundbreaking inventions, which allowed for the recording and viewing of moving pictures, established the framework for motion pictures, including the now standard 35mm film format. After parting ways with Edison in 1895, Dickson co-founded the American Mutoscope and Biograph Company, where his work in large-format filmmaking set new standards in image quality.

In 1899, Dickson turned his lens toward "Savage South Africa", Frank Fillis's ambitious reenactment of colonial battles and African life. Filming the arrival of the show's performers and animals at Southampton, Dickson captured their disembarkation with the precision and clarity characteristic of Biograph's large-format camera. This footage served as a prelude to the spectacle awaiting audiences in London, introducing British viewers to a theatrical production that both fascinated and reinforced imperial ideologies. His work preserved this cultural and colonial exchange moment, immortalising the performers' journey across continents.

Shortly after completing his work on 'Savage South Africa', Dickson travelled to South Africa during the Second Boer War outbreak in late 1899. As one of the earliest war filmmakers, he documented scenes from the conflict, including troop movements, military encampments, and symbolic moments that emphasised the British empire's role in the war. Despite the challenges of filming in a combat zone—ranging from censorship to the technical limitations of early cameras, such as the need for ample light and the bulkiness of equipment—Dickson's footage brought vivid images of the war back to audiences in Britain, shaping perceptions of the conflict.

Dickson's work during this period highlighted his ability to navigate the evolving intersection of technology, storytelling, and propaganda. His films offered a window into the Empire during significant upheaval, using cinema to entertain and influence. While his contributions to early filmmaking remain celebrated for their technical innovation, his involvement in these imperial narratives also underscores the significant role of cinema in shaping public understanding of colonialism and conflict, enlightening us about its power.

Vere Palgrave Stent (1872–1941) was a distinguished South African journalist, war correspondent, theatre critic, playwright, and author. Born in Queenstown, Eastern Cape, he was the son of architect Sydney Stent and the brother of actor Lionel B. Stent. He received his education at St. Andrew's College in Grahamstown.

Stent's career as a war correspondent was notable. In 1897, he reported during the Langberg Rebellion in Bechuanaland, witnessing significant events such as the storming of the Kopje and the death of rebel leader Luka Jantje.

During the Second Boer War (1899–1902), Stent served as the Reuters News Agency correspondent during the Siege of Mafeking from 1899 to 1900. His reporting provided valuable insights into the prolonged 217-day siege, a pivotal event in the war. Stent's presence in Mafeking allowed him to document the daily challenges and resilience of the besieged town.

In 1900, Stent accompanied the 11th Division under General Pole-Carew to Komati Poort, further solidifying his reputation as a dedicated war correspondent. His experiences during these conflicts enriched his later work as a journalist and editor.

Beyond his war correspondence, Stent made significant contributions to South African journalism. In 1903, he acquired and became the editor of the Pretoria News, a position he held until 1920. Under his leadership, the newspaper became a prominent voice in the region.

Stent's multifaceted career also included roles as a theatre critic, playwright, and author, reflecting his diverse interests and talents. His legacy in South African media and literature remains influential, offering a window into the country's historical and cultural landscape during a transformative period.

General Snyman, the Bell-Ringing Baboon

Not all heroes stride boldly into history. Some shuffle in on all fours, armed not with guns but with a bell and a sharp sense of self-preservation. General Snyman, Mafeking's unlikely saviour, was a baboon whose courage and cunning left an indelible mark on the Siege of Mafeking.

During the 217-day siege, this "babjaan" earned his stripes by ringing a bell whenever Boer artillery fired. His warnings gave soldiers and civilians precious seconds to take cover, saving countless lives. Snyman wasn't just an alarm system but a tactician, retreating to safety when his job was done. Nicknamed after the Boer commander General Jacobus Philippus Snyman—who led the siege against Mafeking—the baboon was, as some runners joked, the more reliable of the two generals.

After the siege, General Snyman (the baboon) travelled with British troops to Salisbury Plain in Wiltshire, England—8,000 miles from the veldt. On September 29, 1900, he became the star of an auction, perched on a sale-room counter, munching apples as admirers gathered around him. Sold for 40 guineas to a Mr Wilson, Snyman appeared utterly unimpressed, continuing his apple as if nothing had changed.

Meanwhile, his human namesake faced sharp criticism for his leadership during the siege. Ironically, the baboon who bore his name received more admiration—and far better press.

General Snyman reminds us that heroism isn't about rank or uniform but action. From the dusty streets of Mafeking to the auction rooms of England, his story stands as a curious footnote in history, proving that bravery can take many forms—even if it's holding a bell in one hand and an apple in the other.

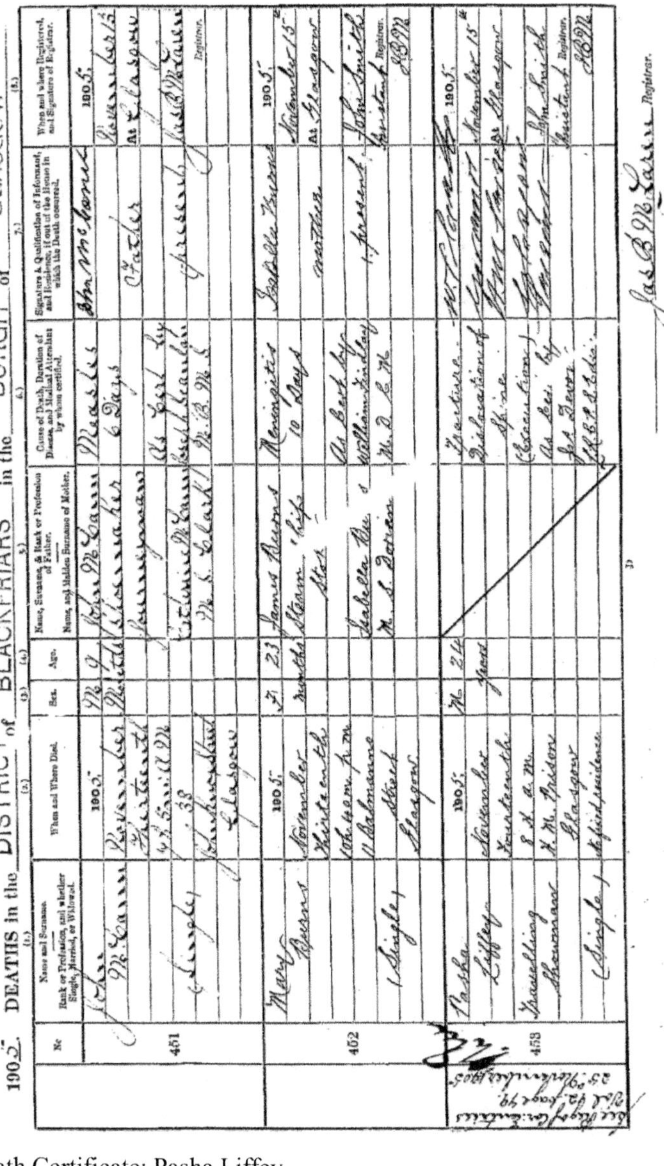

Death Certificate: Pasha Liffey

258

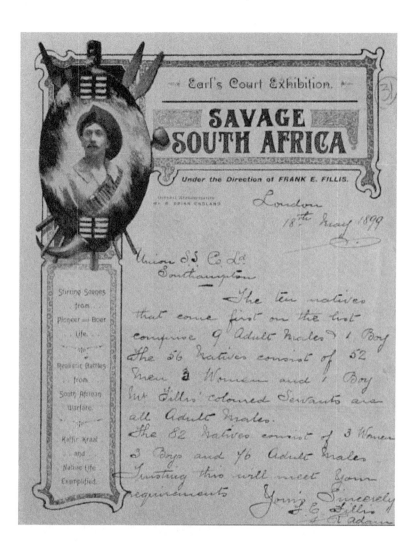

Photos Copyright Crown

Runners, scouts, wagon drivers

The court case of Jan Malhombe

The Ramsbottom Observer, 24 March 1899

Frank Fillis, a South African showman, secures £40,000 to fund his ambitious Savage South Africa show. His vision includes reenacting African battles, showcasing "native warriors," and exhibiting exotic animals. The funding allows him to charter the passenger vessel SS Goth to transport performers and animals to England.

Shipping Records, 25 March 1899

The SS Goth departs South Africa, laden with lions, elephants, ponies, and 150 performers. The manifest includes Matabele and Zulu warriors, Swazi dancers, and Basuto boys, among them Pasha Liffey. This journey symbolises a blending of cultures but also underscores the exploitative nature of colonial exhibitions, prompting reflection on the cultural implications of such displays.

Hull Evening News, 19 April 1899

The SS Goth docks in Southampton after nearly a month at sea. Reporters flock to document the arrival of what they term the "largest African contingent ever to reach British shores." Performers and animals are paraded for inspection, creating a spectacle even before the show begins.

The Morning Post, 20 April 1899

A detailed account describes the performers travelling by train from Southampton to London. Crowds gather at the stations to catch a glimpse of the "Zulu chiefs" and "Matabele warriors." The train journey becomes part of the spectacle, with press coverage amplifying the excitement.

Evening Chronicle, 21 April 1899

The drama unfolds when elephants escape their enclosures during transit. The animals stroll down the tracks, kicking train cars and causing delays, cementing the show's reputation as both chaotic and thrilling.

Taunton Courier, 26 April 1899

The performers and animals arrive at Earl's Court, greeted by enthusiastic crowds. The article highlights the event's symbolic importance, framing it as a celebration of Britain's colonial achievements.

The Times, 8 May 1899

Savage South Africa opens to critical and widespread acclaim. The highlight, Wilson's Last Stand, reenacts the Shangani Patrol, a battle in which Matabele warriors surrounded and killed British forces. The show blends drama with imperial propaganda, romanticising British heroism.

The Standard, 23 May 1899

Reports document record-breaking attendance figures, with over 92,000 visitors daily by late May. Crowds are drawn to The Kraal, a constructed African village where performers interact with guests. While popular, The Kraal also faces criticism for commodifying African culture.

Western Morning News, 24 May 1899

Chiefs from the show hold an Indaba at Earl's Court to celebrate Queen Victoria's birthday. The event, orchestrated for publicity, showcases traditional dances and blessings, emphasising loyalty to the Crown.

Reynolds's Newspaper, 9 May 1899

Joseph Chamberlain, Secretary of State for the Colonies, publicly criticises the show for exploiting indigenous peoples. However, members of the Royal Family, including the Prince of Wales, endorse the exhibition, shielding it from broader political backlash.

The Sunday People, 14 May 1899

Reports emerge of scandals within The Kraal, including alleged romantic liaisons between visitors and performers. These rumours generate public fascination but tarnish the show's reputation.

The Standard, 6 July 1899

A detailed description of Wilson's Last Stand highlights its theatrical grandeur, complete with gunfire, cavalry charges, and dramatic deaths. The article notes that some performers are veterans of African battles, lending authenticity to the reenactment.

The Manchester Courier, 26 June 1900

Rising tensions among the performers culminate in a fight between a Swazi performer and a Basuto boy, believed to be Pasha Liffey. The altercation reflects broader issues of racial hierarchy within the camp.

Twelve Cape Boys are sent back to South Africa due to disciplinary actions.

The Westminster Budget, 7 July 1900

A feature article exposes the racial and social divides among the show's participants. It describes the performers' living conditions and notes the disparities between African and European participants.

Liverpool Echo, 3 July 1900

A violent brawl breaks out between Boer and Zulu performers, underscoring ongoing tensions rooted in South Africa's colonial conflicts. The incident highlights the challenges of maintaining cohesion within such a diverse troupe.

Manchester Evening News, 27 December 1901

Prince Lobengula, a prominent figure in the show, is arrested for being drunk and disorderly. His arrest exemplifies the struggles faced by many performers after the show's dissolution as they grapple with poverty and marginalisation.

Prisoner's Log, October–November 1905

During his imprisonment, Pasha Liffey reflects on his life, recalling his early years in Lesotho, his work with horses in England, and his participation in the Savage South Africa show. The logs describe him as restless, depressed, and deeply prayerful.

Recommended Reading

- The Boer War Diary of Sol Plaatje
- Kitty and The Prince – Ben Shephard
- Sol Plaatje – A Life of Solomon Tshekisho Plaatje – Brian P Willan
- Frank Fillis – The Story Of A Circus Legend – Floris van der Merwe

Printed in Great Britain
by Amazon